OCR A LEVEL

RELIGIOUS STUDIES

Religion and Ethics

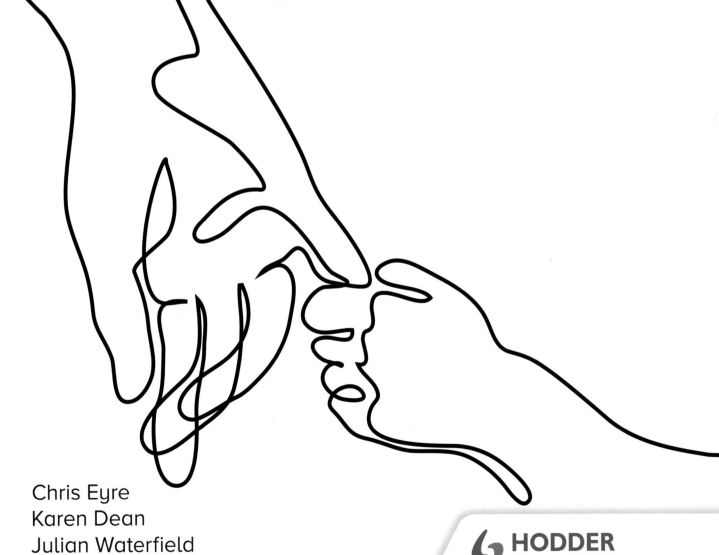

Chris Eyre
Karen Dean
Julian Waterfield

HODDER
EDUCATION
AN HACHETTE UK COMPANY

The Publishers would like to thank the following for permission to reproduce copyright material.

Photo credits

p.1 *tl* © Djomas/stock.adobe.com; *tr* © Kitthanes/stock.adobe.com; *b* © Karandaev/stock.adobe.com; **p.4** © The Granger Collection/TopFoto; **p.10** © Monkey Business/stock.adobe.com; **p.29** *l* © Ian West/PA Archive/PA Images; *m* © Keystone/Zuma/Shutterstock; *r* © Shutterstock; **p.30** Immanuel Kant. Stipple engraving by J. Chapman, 1812. Credit: Wellcome Collection. Attribution 4.0 International (CC BY 4.0); **p.44** © Geogphotos/Alamy Stock Photo; **p.46** © TopFoto.co.uk; **p.75** *t* © Renaud Rebardy/Alamy Stock Photo; *m* © WavebreakMediaMicro/stock.adobe.com; *b* © Andrew Rowland/PRiME Media Images/Alamy Stock Photo; **p.77** © Archive PL/Alamy Stock Photo; **p.84** © Ray Tang/Shutterstock; **p.93** © Gtranquillity/stock.adobe.com; **p.111** *t* © Vudi Xhymshiti/ZUMA Wire/Shutterstock; *b* © Gallo Images Avusa/Joe Sefale/Getty images; **p.125** © The Independent; **p.128** © Nathaniel Noir/Alamy Stock Photo; **p.130** ©Paul Lovichi Photography/Alamy Stock Photo

Acknowledgements

Every effort has been made to trace all copyright holders, but if any have been inadvertently overlooked, the Publishers will be pleased to make the necessary arrangements at the first opportunity.

Although every effort has been made to ensure that website addresses are correct at time of going to press, Hodder Education cannot be held responsible for the content of any website mentioned in this book. It is sometimes possible to find a relocated web page by typing in the address of the home page for a website in the URL window of your browser.

Hachette UK's policy is to use papers that are natural, renewable and recyclable products and made from wood grown in well-managed forests and other controlled sources. The logging and manufacturing processes are expected to conform to the environmental regulations of the country of origin.

Orders: please contact Bookpoint Ltd, 130 Park Drive, Milton Park, Abingdon, Oxon OX14 4SE. Telephone: +44 (0)1235 827827. Fax: +44 (0)1235 400401. Email education@bookpoint.co.uk Lines are open from 9 a.m. to 5 p.m., Monday to Saturday, with a 24-hour message answering service. You can also order through our website: www.hoddereducation.co.uk

ISBN: 9781510479951

© Chris Eyre, Julian Waterfield and Karen Dean 2020

First published in 2020 by

Hodder Education, An Hachette UK Company, Carmelite House, 50 Victoria Embankment, London EC4Y 0DZ

www.hoddereducation.co.uk

Impression number   10 9 8 7 6 5 4 3 2 1

Year   2024 2023 2022 2021 2020

Cover photo © By Valenty - stock.adobe.com

Illustrations by Aptara; Barking Dog Art

Typeset in India by Aptara

Printed in Italy

A catalogue record for this title is available from the British Library.

FSC
www.fsc.org

MIX
Paper from responsible sources
FSC™ C104740

Contents

About the course

How to use this book

This book is designed to be used alongside class teaching and your wider reading. It aims to introduce the big ethical topics covered by the specification, which is a broad introduction to the subject of ethics and religion.

Each chapter begins with a 'way in' to the topic and prints the relevant part of the specification. Then there follows a series of double page spreads that explore at least one big question that you need to study for your A or AS Level exam. Remember that if a word is found on the specification then it can turn up in a question. Make sure you are clear on every word and phrase before you go into the exam.

It is sometimes tempting to focus all your learning on knowing different facts but 60 per cent of your assessment will come from your ability to analyse and evaluate a particular question. This book aims to keep you focused on that skill and to provide you with enough knowledge, rather than swamping you with it.

At the end of each double page there is a set of questions. The *Core* questions test your engagement with the material in that section. The *Stretch* questions require you to think outside the box a bit and sometimes to do some further research, usually using the internet. The *Challenge* questions take you beyond the specification and help you to think more about the place of the topic in the context of ethics as a whole.

Each chapter ends with a review section, some further whole topic questions, including more extension material and a debate you might hold as a class, and then a focus on one aspect of essay-writing skills.

How to study this course

The most important thing to do is to engage with the material you cover in class! Ask questions, listen to your classmates (and the teacher!) and make excellent notes (in your own words so that you 'own' the material). Outside of class, look up anything you've found tricky in class and don't be afraid of being interested by a topic and just reading more widely, whether it is a book from the library or on the internet. Just be careful with websites and make sure you understand who wrote the material – some websites are written by religious believers or others who are arguing strongly for a given point of view and some A Level websites are written by students, rather than teachers or experts in the topic.

The most important thing you must do is to write essays. You will be assessed purely by essay in the final exams and you need to practise these as a skill, much like you would a musical instrument. Put all your effort into your essays and when you get them returned, reflect on what you can do next time. Don't just read the teacher's comments and put them away but use the feedback to set yourself a target – something specific to improve on in the next essay. Each chapter has a 'Get practising' section at the end that will give you an insight into essay skills.

Finally, make sure you enjoy the course! Some topics will engage you more than others but choosing to study A Levels is a positive choice and the course should be filled with lots of fun.

Assessment

OCR Religious Studies assesses you across two 'Assessment Objectives':

- AO1 – knowledge and understanding – the facts needed to be able to engage with the topics (40% of the marks)
- AO2 – analysis and evaluation – making those facts your own and being able to think critically about them (60% of the marks).

All essays will be given a mark for each of these AOs separately, but you need to practise writing essays that combine the two throughout the essay – your teacher will give you support in structuring these.

Assessment Objective 1: Knowledge and understanding

Marks for AO1 come from being able to **select the right information** which contributes to your **answering of the question**. The best essays come from being **precise** in the information (not waffly) and making sure that everything is explained **concisely** – i.e. you write enough and not everything you know about a topic. Show the examiner that you are in control.

Assessment Objective 2: Analysis and evaluation

At AO2, you are **arguing** to explore **all sides of a question**. Often this will be points for and against but the highest marks come from those candidates who understand that all strengths and weaknesses themselves have advantages and disadvantages. Never leave an argument hanging in an essay, **unexplored**.

See overleaf for the mark scheme criteria for AO1 and AO2.

OCR A Level Religious Studies: OCR maintains the qualification specification on the OCR website. You should always check for the latest version and any updates. https://www.ocr.org.uk/qualifications/as-and-a-level/religious-studies-h173-h573-from-2016/

Level	AO1 mark scheme description
6 (14–16)	An excellent demonstration of knowledge and understanding in response to the question: • fully comprehends the demands of, and focusses on, the question throughout • excellent selection of relevant material which is skilfully used • accurate and highly detailed knowledge which demonstrates deep understanding through a complex and nuanced approach to the material used • thorough, accurate and precise use of technical terms and vocabulary in context • extensive range of scholarly views, academic approaches, and/or sources of wisdom and authority are used to demonstrate knowledge and understanding.
5 (11–13) (AS: 13–15)	A very good demonstration of knowledge and understanding in response to the question: • focuses on the precise question throughout • very good selection of relevant material which is used appropriately • accurate and detailed knowledge which demonstrates very good understanding through either the breadth or depth of material used • accurate and appropriate use of technical terms and subject vocabulary • a very good range of scholarly views, academic approaches, and/or sources of wisdom and authority are used to demonstrate knowledge and understanding.
4 (8–10) (AS: 10–12)	A good demonstration of knowledge and understanding in response to the question: • addresses the question well • good selection of relevant material, used appropriately on the whole • mostly accurate knowledge which demonstrates good understanding of the material used, which should have reasonable amounts of depth or breadth • mostly accurate and appropriate use of technical terms and subject vocabulary • a good range of scholarly views, academic approaches, and/or sources of wisdom and authority are used to demonstrate knowledge and understanding.
3 (5–7) (AS: 7–9)	A satisfactory demonstration of knowledge and understanding in response to the question: • generally addresses the question • mostly sound selection of mostly relevant material • some accurate knowledge which demonstrates sound understanding through the material used, which might however be lacking in depth or breadth • generally appropriate use of technical terms and subject vocabulary • a satisfactory range of scholarly views, academic approaches, and/or sources of wisdom and authority are used to demonstrate knowledge and understanding with only partial success.
2 (3–4) (AS: 4–6)	A basic demonstration of knowledge and understanding in response to the question: • might address the general topic rather than the question directly • limited selection of partially relevant material • some accurate, but limited, knowledge which demonstrates partial understanding • some accurate, but limited, use of technical terms and appropriate subject vocabulary • a limited range of scholarly views, academic approaches, and/or sources of wisdom and authority are used to demonstrate knowledge and understanding with little success.
1 (1–2) (AS: 1–3)	A weak demonstration of knowledge and understanding in response to the question: • almost completely ignores the question • very little relevant material selected • knowledge very limited, demonstrating little understanding • very little use of technical terms or subject vocabulary • very little or no use of scholarly views, academic approaches and/or sources of wisdom and authority to demonstrate knowledge and understanding.
0(0)	No creditworthy response.

Level	AO2 mark scheme description
6 **(21–24)**	An excellent demonstration of analysis and evaluation in response to the question: ● excellent, clear and successful argument ● confident and insightful critical analysis and detailed evaluation of the issue ● views skilfully and clearly stated, coherently developed and justified ● answers the question set precisely throughout ● thorough, accurate and precise use of technical terms and vocabulary in context ● extensive range of scholarly views, academic approaches and sources of wisdom and authority used to support analysis and evaluation. *Assessment of Extended Response: There is an excellent line of reasoning, well-developed and sustained, which is coherent, relevant and logically structured.*
5 **(17–20)** **(AS: 13–15)**	A very good demonstration of analysis and evaluation in response to the question: ● clear argument which is mostly successful ● successful and clear analysis and evaluation ● views very well stated, coherently developed and justified ● answers the question set competently ● accurate and appropriate use of technical terms and subject vocabulary ● a very good range of scholarly views, academic approaches and sources of wisdom and authority used to support analysis and evaluation. *Assessment of Extended Response: There is a well-developed and sustained line of reasoning which is coherent, relevant and logically structured.*
4 **(13–16)** **(AS: 10–12)**	A good demonstration of analysis and evaluation in response to the question: ● argument is generally successful and clear ● generally successful analysis and evaluation ● views well stated, with some development and justification ● answers the question set well ● mostly accurate and appropriate use of technical terms and subject vocabulary ● a good range of scholarly views, academic approaches and sources of wisdom and authority are used to support analysis and evaluation. *Assessment of Extended Response: There is a well–developed line of reasoning which is clear, relevant and logically structured.*
3 **(9–12)** **(AS: 7–9)**	A satisfactory demonstration of analysis and/evaluation in response to the question: ● some successful argument ● partially successful analysis and evaluation ● views asserted but often not fully justified ● mostly answers the set question ● generally appropriate use of technical terms and subject vocabulary ● a satisfactory range of scholarly views, academic approaches and sources of wisdom and authority are used to support analysis and evaluation with only partial success. *Assessment of Extended Response: There is a line of reasoning presented which is mostly relevant and which has some structure.*
2 **(5–8)** **(AS: 4–6)**	A basic demonstration of analysis and evaluation in response to the question: ● some argument attempted, not always successful ● little successful analysis and evaluation ● views asserted but with little justification ● only partially answers the question ● some accurate, but limited, use of technical terms and appropriate subject vocabulary ● a limited range of scholarly views, academic approaches and sources of wisdom and authority are used to support analysis and evaluation with little success. *Assessment of Extended Response: There is a line of reasoning which has some relevance and which is presented with limited structure.*
1 **(1–4)** **(AS: 1–3)**	A weak demonstration of analysis and evaluation in response to the question: ● very little argument attempted ● very little successful analysis and evaluation ● views asserted with very little justification ● unsuccessful in answering the question ● very little use of technical terms or subject vocabulary ● very little or no use of scholarly views, academic approaches and sources of wisdom and authority to support analysis and evaluation. *Assessment of Extended Response: The information is communicated in a basic/unstructured way.*
0(0)	No creditworthy response.

The exam

If you are studying the full A Level then you will sit three exams at the end of the course – one in Philosophy, one in Ethics and one in the religion you are studying. Each exam will give you four questions and you need to choose three – this means the best advice is that it is not possible to drop a topic as sometimes you end up talking about more than one topic in an essay. The exams are two hours long and so each essay has 40 minutes – two minutes to plan, three minutes for your introduction, four chunky paragraphs and about three minutes for the conclusion.

If you are studying for the AS Level then each of your three exams will be 1 hour 15 minutes with just over 35 minutes for each essay.

Revision

Revising for an exam is a personal thing and you will know from your GCSEs what has worked for you – some people prefer words, some mind maps, some flash cards and so on. However, don't forget that you will be dealing with a vast quantity of information compared to your GCSEs over more than one subject area and so the techniques you used at GCSE won't necessarily be the right ones to use at this level. Use every opportunity to get your revision notes sorted out before the actual exam year – your internal mock exams, your class tests and so on. The more you have done through the course, the easier you will find those final exams. Ultimately, when you get to the exams, you do not want to be picking up these textbooks again! You want all you need to be in one set of organised notes so that you can keep calm and focused as you commit them to memory.

Remember even during revision that you must keep the focus on AO2. Some students find it helpful to learn material by starting with strengths and weaknesses of areas and moving from there onto the core AO1 knowledge.

Further reading

The same author team have published other books you might find helpful in your course. There are workbooks published for each of the three papers with questions to help you structure your thought for each topic. The *My Revision Notes* series of A Level revision guides written for this OCR course condense the information from the course even further. Also, the book *Aiming for an A in A-level Religious Studies* can guide you through the course and give you study skill ideas and essay technique suggestions. All these books can be found on the Hodder website, www.hoddereducation.co.uk.

Introduction to ethics

Aim

Gain an overview of key debates and terms within ethics.

Starter

On a copy of the diagram below, sort the following actions: giving to charity; murder; going for a walk; fox hunting; telling lies; keeping promises; kindness; singing a song; torturing people; stealing.

Compare your answers to those given by a classmate.

Are there any that you disagree on?

Are there any that do not fit in any of the three sections?

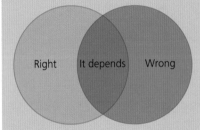

What is ethics?

Ethics can be defined as the branch of knowledge that deals with moral principles; it is the study of the moral principles that govern how we act or behave. As we saw in the Starter activity, there are many things we do that are not governed by ethics – our eating, walking and conversations are not usually subject to the categories of right and wrong. Ethics is about those actions or behaviours where the categories of right and wrong may be applied.

It is worth noting that ethics is not the same as study of law. While murder is both morally and legally wrong, telling a lie in most circumstances is not against the law, but could be viewed as morally wrong. Equally, there may be occasions where someone may argue that the law is wrong and there is a moral duty to disobey it, for example during civil rights protests on racial equality.

Ethics is not the same as customs and culture. There are different customs for how we greet others (a kiss on the cheek or a handshake, for example), but to fail to shake hands with someone is not usually seen as morally wrong.

Types of ethical questions

There are three main levels of ethical questions.

Meta-ethics: From the Greek 'meta', meaning above and beyond. The study of the meaning of ethical concepts, e.g. what does 'good' mean? Does it actually exist?

↑

Normative ethics: Considers ethical theories that give advice on how we ought to behave.

↑

Applied ethics: Discusses specific problems in ethics, e.g. whether euthanasia should be permitted.

- Chapters 1–4 of this book examine normative ethics. The theories of natural law, situation ethics, Kantian ethics and utilitarianism all aim to provide general guidance and rules on how to act.
- Chapters 5, 6 and 9 examine three issues in applied ethics: euthanasia, business ethics and sexual ethics. Each of these topics considers how the normative theories might help to solve the issues.
- Chapter 7 considers meta-ethics, and Chapter 8 examines the issue of conscience – a consideration that might affect ethical discussion at each of the three levels of questioning.

Approaches to normative ethics

In normative ethics, theories are often characterised as being **absolutist** or **relativist**. An absolutist believes that moral rules are fixed and apply at all times and in all places. A relativist believes that moral rules are not fixed, but are instead dependent on situation or culture.

Ethical theories can also be characterised as **deontological** or **teleological**. A deontological ethic concentrates on whether the action itself is good, for example is it right or wrong to steal? A teleological ethic judges the rightness of an action by its consequence, for example it may be acceptable to steal if your family is starving.

Typically, natural law and Kantian ethics are absolutist and deontological. Utilitarianism and situation ethics are relativist and teleological. However, the division of ethical theories into deontological and teleological is a generalisation. The desire to put labels on to theories and categorise them into neat boxes is largely a twentieth-century development. It is entirely possible to argue that natural law is teleological and that rule utilitarianism is not completely relativist.

Key terms

Absolutism In ethics, the idea that right and wrong is fixed at all times and for all people

Relativism The idea that what is right or wrong is not fixed, but is dependent on situation or culture

Deontological An ethic that is focused on the rightness or wrongness of the action itself, often using the idea of duty

Teleological The idea that goodness is determined by the outcome of an action

Activities

Core

1 What is the key difference between absolute and relative ethics?

2 What is the key difference between deontological and teleological ethics?

3 What is the difference between normative ethics and meta-ethics?

Stretch

4 In the Ring of Gyges example, Plato argues that it is important to do the right thing even if we could get away with doing the wrong thing.

Write a paragraph assessing whether he is right. What do you think and why?

5 A law student says, 'There is no need to study ethics, we have the law to tell us what is right and wrong.' How would you answer them?

Challenge

6 Choose one of the thinkers on the ethics timeline and research their views. As a class you could research different thinkers and briefly present their ideas. This will introduce some of the thinkers you will meet during this topic and provide some context and background on their ideas.

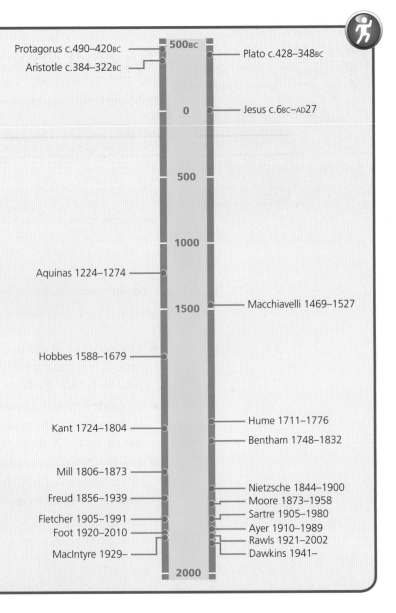

Protagorus c.490–420BC

Aristotle c.384–322BC

500BC

Plato c.428–348BC

0

Jesus c.6BC–AD27

500

1000

Aquinas 1224–1274

1500

Macchiavelli 1469–1527

Hobbes 1588–1679

Kant 1724–1804

Hume 1711–1776

Bentham 1748–1832

Mill 1806–1873

Freud 1856–1939

Nietzsche 1844–1900

Moore 1873–1958

Sartre 1905–1980

Fletcher 1905–1991

Foot 1920–2010

Ayer 1910–1989

Rawls 1921–2002

Dawkins 1941–

MacIntyre 1929–

2000

Natural law

One way of approaching ethical decision-making is the idea that right and wrong can be decided based on whether something fulfils its purpose. Thomas Aquinas argues that everything, including people, has a *telos* (purpose) and that whether actions are good depends upon whether the purpose is fulfilled.

Engage

Look at the photos, and copy and complete the table.

What is it?	What is its purpose?	How would you decide if it was good?
Chair		
Knife		
Human being		

For natural law thinkers, the second and third columns of the table are linked. Whether something is good depends on whether it achieves its purpose. If the chair collapsed under you when you sat on it, you could not describe it as a good chair. Aristotle's theory of the four causes (in the Philosophy component of the course) suggests that everything has a final cause or '*telos*'. Everything and everyone should aim to fulfil their *telos*.

You will probably find that the final row of the table is the hardest! Discuss in pairs what you think the purpose of human beings might be. Review Aristotle's theory of the four causes if you have already covered it in the Philosophy component.

▲ What makes any of these things good?

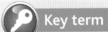

Key term

Telos Greek word meaning the purpose or end (as in aim) of something

The specification

Content	Key knowledge
Aquinas' natural law, including: ● *telos* ● the four tiers of law ● the precepts	● Origins of the significant concept of *telos* in Aristotle and its religious development in the writing of Aquinas ● What they are and how they are related: 1 Eternal law: The principles by which God made and controls the universe and which are fully known only to God 2 Divine law: The law of God revealed in the Bible, particularly in the Ten Commandments and the Sermon on the Mount 3 Natural law: The moral law of God within human nature that is discoverable through the use of reason 4 Human law: The laws of nations ● What they are and how they are related: • The key precept (do good, avoid evil) • Five primary precepts (preservation of life, ordering of society, worship of God, education of children, reproduction) • Secondary precepts

Learners should have the opportunity to discuss issues raised by Aquinas' theory of natural law, including:
- whether or not natural law provides a helpful method of moral decision-making
- whether or not a judgement about something being good, bad, right or wrong can be based on its success or failure in achieving its *telos*
- whether or not the universe as a whole is designed with a *telos*, or human nature has an orientation towards the good
- whether or not the doctrine of double effect can be used to justify an action, such as killing someone as an act of self-defence.

1.1 What are the key ideas of natural law?

 Aim

Learn about the key ideas of natural law ethics and how these help followers make moral decisions.

 Starter

An evil alien race has taken over planet Earth. It plans to wipe out human life, but will spare it if you can show that there is something unique and special about human beings that means they are worth keeping alive. What could you say that would save humanity?

 Key term

Synderesis The innate principle or natural disposition directing a person towards good and away from evil

 Key quote

'This is the first precept of law, that "good is to be done and pursued, and evil is to be avoided". All other precepts of the natural law are based upon this'.
(Aquinas, *Summa Theologica*)

Telos

Aristotle and Aquinas argue that human beings have a unique *telos*. For Aristotle, this is found in rational thought. While we share many features with other creatures on the planet – such as the ability to reproduce, to grow and to feel emotions – we are unique in having the ability to reason and reflect. In exercising our reason, we are flourishing and achieving our *telos*.

Aquinas develops this idea. As humans, we are uniquely able to reflect on our moral behaviour and to consider whether the things we are doing are good or bad. For Aquinas the main moral rule is that we 'do good and avoid evil'. This is known as the **synderesis** rule. All other moral rules are taken from this.

Primary and secondary precepts

Aquinas believes that when we reflect on our *telos* and understand the key rule, there are five primary precepts or rules that follow from this. Aquinas believes that these are self-evident and are things that we are naturally inclined to pursue.

1 **Preservation of innocent life:** Aquinas argues that we are to preserve life. It is evident that life is important, both our own and that of others. It is natural and reasonable for a person to be concerned with 'Preserving its own being and ... preserving human life'.

2 **To reproduce:** It is also rational to ensure that life continues and this is the main purpose of sexual intercourse.

3 **Education**, particularly education of the young: Humans are intellectual creatures and it is natural for us to learn.

4 **To live in an ordered society:** We are social beings and it is good to live in an ordered society where it is possible to fulfil our purpose.

5 **To worship God:** We are also spiritual beings and we should recognise God as the source of life and live in a way that pleases him.

The primary precepts are absolute and universal, but they are general statements about what is good for humans – they do not necessarily tell us exactly how to act. Aquinas therefore suggests that secondary precepts are needed. These are more specific rules that can be deduced from the primary precepts. For example, if preservation of life is a primary precept, then we can deduce that killing a fellow human is wrong. The primary precepts are fixed – these are what is good for humans. The secondary precepts may have some flexibility as we have to consider how the primary precepts are to be applied in each situation.

The four tiers of law

Aquinas sees the universe as being created with a God-given order. This order is also seen in the moral law that is built into the universe. Aquinas argues that there are the following four levels of law.

The eternal law

The eternal law is the law as known in the mind of God. It is his knowledge of what is right and wrong. Aquinas refers to the effects of eternal law in terms of moving all things towards their end and purpose; God's wisdom is reflected in his creation. These are moral truths that we, at a human level, may be unable to fathom.

The divine law

The divine law refers to the law revealed by God through the commands and teachings through revelation, for example in scripture. These include the Ten Commandments and the moral teachings of Jesus such as in the Sermon on the Mount. While Aquinas primarily believes that law is rational rather than revealed, he believes that the divine laws revealed by God are reasonable, that we could work them out.

Natural law

Natural law is the moral thinking that we are all able to do, whether or not we have had the divine revelation of scripture. All humans have the capacity to consider and work out the moral rules necessary for achieving our purpose. We have been given this capacity by God. This involves a rational reflection on our human nature, considering how we might 'do good and avoid evil' and working out secondary precepts for situations.

Human law

Human laws are the customs and practices of a society. They are devised by governments and by societies. Ideally, government laws should be based on what we reason from natural law.

Ultimately, Aquinas sees the relationship between these four laws as hierarchical, with the other laws all ultimately relying on the eternal law.

> ### Key quote
>
> 'Man is bound to obey secular rulers to the extent that the order of justice requires ... if they command unjust things, their subjects are not obliged to obey them.'
> (Aquinas, *Summa Theologica*)

Activities

Core

1 What are the five primary precepts?
2 How does natural law relate to the laws that are in the Bible?
3 What does Aquinas believe about whether we need to obey the laws of our country?

Stretch

4 How do Aristotle and Aquinas differ on the idea of *telos*?

5 Suggest a possible secondary precept for each of the five primary precepts.

Challenge

6 Find out about the philosophy of Stoicism. How did this Ancient Greek school affect understandings of natural law?

1.2 Is natural law a helpful method of making moral decisions?

Aim

Understand how to apply natural law and consider whether it is a useful approach for moral decision-making.

Issue	Most relevant primary precept	Specific secondary precept
Contraception	Reproduce	'Do not use artificial contraception'
Marriage		
Euthanasia		
Abortion		

Starter

Following the example completed in the table below, use the knowledge you have gained from pages 2 and 3 to apply natural law to the suggested issues.

You will be able to check your answers as you read later sections of this book.

Tip

One common error or over-simplification is to use natural law and Roman Catholicism as if they are the same thing. While it is true that Roman Catholic ethics is based on a natural law approach, it also takes seriously the Bible and the tradition and teaching of the Church. Equally, at times Catholicism, influenced by the manualists, has taken quite a narrow interpretation of natural law and is certainly not the only way that natural law can be read.

Meet the thinker

▲ Thomas Aquinas (1224–74)

Biography: Born to a wealthy Italian family, Aquinas became a monk. This was much to his family's disgust and they even tried to kidnap him at one point. He devoted his life to philosophy, his *Summa Theologica* being a vast and influential text. He was declared a saint in 1323.

Key ideas: Aquinas attempts to harmonise the ideas of Aristotle, whom he refers to as 'THE philosopher', and the teachings of Christianity. His sense of regularity and order in the universe influences both his arguments for God and his natural law ethics.

Appears in: Natural law, euthanasia, conscience, sexual ethics, and philosophy topics such as the cosmological argument, the teleological argument and religious language.

Interpreting the natural law

Aquinas' use of primary and secondary precepts can be viewed in different ways. For Aquinas, the secondary precepts are possible applications rather than hard and fast rules. Yet the Catholic Church, particularly a school of thought known as the manualists, has made quite fixed secondary precepts – for example, an absolute rejection of all artificial contraception given that the primary precept is reproduction. It is often this view of natural law that critics have in mind when suggesting that natural law is too rigid or outdated.

A differing perspective on natural law is given by thinkers who wish to go back to Aristotle. For Aristotle, the aim of human beings is *eudaimonia* – a Greek word that can be translated as fulfilment or flourishing. As previously stated, our unique *telos* as human beings is to do with our ability to reason; it is this that makes us fully human. Aristotle's own ethical ideas (known as virtue ethics) argue that we have to develop good character traits to enable us to fulfil our function and reach *eudaimonia*.

Modern natural law thinkers, such as Robert George and John Finnis have developed ideas of natural law that owe as much to Aristotle as they do to Aquinas. Finnis (1940–) is interested in natural law both as an ethical theory and as a philosophy of law. He uses Aristotle's idea of practical reasoning or **phronesis** to suggest that there are certain basic goods of

Key term

Phronesis An ancient Greek Philosophical term meaning wisdom or intelligence, mainly used to refer to practical wisdom and moral decision-making

Key term

Naturalistic fallacy The mistake of defining moral terms with reference to non-moral or natural terms

human flourishing, such as knowledge, play, work, aesthetic experience, friendship and spirituality. From these, more specific rules can be put forward, such as pursuing basic goods for all, desiring the common good of the community and acting according to one's conscience. Finnis argues that although we should think about the consequences of our actions, we should not think that the end justifies the means.

Analyse and evaluate

Natural law can be seen as a helpful way of making moral decisions because:	*Natural law is unhelpful as an approach to moral decision-making because:*
The primary precepts are not particularly controversial. They are goods that are valued by all societies, both present and past, *but* ... (See the first reason in the unhelpful column.)	(From the first reason in the helpful column) ... it can be argued that basic goods vary far more across societies than is generally realised. When these are taken to the level of secondary precepts, it becomes obvious that there are different attitudes to the value of life, which gods should be worshipped and how many people can be involved in marriages.
The primary precepts in particular lead natural law to predominantly be an absolutist ethical theory. This means that there is a clarity to its judgements.	As an absolutist theory, natural law can at times appear too legalistic and fixed on obeying the rules, particularly when there are very obvious negative consequences. The spread of HIV/Aids in Africa as a result of Catholic teaching opposing contraception is one particularly unpleasant example. However, it might be argued that this is to do with how the theory has been interpreted rather than anything to do with the theory itself.
Unlike other absolutist approaches to ethics, there is some flexibility in terms of the application of secondary precepts that may take situation into account. It has to be pointed out, however, that some interpreters of natural law, particularly within the Catholic tradition, have not always been flexible.	Natural law commits the **naturalistic fallacy** of observing what happens in the world and assuming that this is what must happen. It attempts to define moral values in non-moral terms (see Chapter 7 on meta-ethics).
Natural law leads to a belief in certain rights that exist regardless of context. The value of life, the right to education and to live in peace are seen as part of the natural order of the world.	There is a tension between the clarity of the primary precepts and the flexibility of the secondary precepts. The catechism does not recognise this difficulty in its claim that the natural law is 'universal in its approach' and the 'application of the natural law varies greatly'.
Natural law affirms the importance of reason; humans are made in God's image and possess the rational capacity to work out right and wrong by observation of the world.	See also the discussion of *telos* on the next pages for further issues with natural law.

Activities

Core

1 Explain two strengths of natural law ethics.
2 Explain two weaknesses of natural law ethics.
3 How have some strict Roman Catholics (the manualists) differed from the views of Thomas Aquinas in how natural law is interpreted?

Stretch

4 Explain what is meant by the naturalistic fallacy.
5 To what extent do you think that the primary precepts are shared by all societies? Justify your answer.

Challenge

6 Find out more about different schools of thought within natural law using websites such as the Internet Encyclopedia of Philosophy and the Stanford University Philosophy site. Do you think any of the approaches is more convincing? Does one of the approaches address some of the weaknesses above?

1.3 Can right and wrong be based on the idea of *telos*?

Aim

Learn about *telos* and whether it can be a good basis for an ethical theory.

Starter

Read the dialogue below. What are your initial thoughts about whether human beings can also have purpose?

Vic: This meal is lovely, but I do wish you would use your knife not your hands.

Rick: Why does it matter?

Vic: Cutting your food is what your knife is for. It has an obvious purpose.

Rick: It has other uses too; I use it to stir my tea when I can't find the spoon. And what does it matter if I use my hands to eat food rather than to write, type or shake hands?

Vic: But that isn't the knife's purpose, you can't just use it for other things. It was made by its designer for the purpose of cutting food. It is what Aquinas refers to as telos.

Rick: Tell us more – or should I say, telos more!

Vic: Everything in the universe has a purpose and we can establish whether something is good based on whether it achieves that purpose. A knife that does not cut is not a good knife.

Rick: I'm not sure everything has a purpose. Things seem to have lots of purposes. Take human beings, for instance.

Vic: Aquinas would say we are made by God for a purpose – he has five primary precepts.

Rick: He is assuming God exists. In any case, the knife starts as an idea, is made and has no choice except to be a knife. We are different – we exist and then we choose our purpose.

Vic: Unlike this knife, you can be quite blunt at times.

I'm trapped in this job for the next 20 years

▲ Sartre argues that we always have freedom even if we fool ourselves into thinking this is not the case

Key term

Existentialism A philosophical movement that stresses the uniqueness of each human individual by arguing that existence comes before essence

Aquinas and *telos*

Aquinas believes that there is a fixed human nature. We are made in the image of God and have a clear purpose or *telos*. Aquinas and Aristotle are 'essentialists'. There is something that it is to be human that we cannot change, even if we wish to. That we aim to fulfil the primary precepts – and that it is morally right for us to do so – is built into our human nature.

Sartre's existentialism

In contrast to the essentialist position is the **existentialist** view, which is associated with thinkers such as Jean-Paul Sartre (1905–80). Sartre's view is that objects may have a fixed nature – for example, a knife starts as an idea in its maker's mind, is made for a purpose and must carry out that purpose. Human beings, however, are fundamentally different. As an atheist, Sartre believes that humans could only have purpose or *telos* if they had been made by God. He believes we come into existence first and then we must decide for ourselves what our essence is – in other words, what we are for.

Sartre argues that we have a tendency to deny our freedom and behave as if we were mere objects. He calls this living in bad faith. In a famous example, he describes a café waiter who in over-exaggerating his gestures and movements is 'playing the role of a waiter', as if there is nothing else he could possibly do. Sartre argues this is not the case, however: his essence is not fixed, he can choose different employment.

Analyse and evaluate

Natural law is right to base ideas of right and wrong on telos *because:*	*Natural law is wrong to base ideas of right and wrong on* telos *because:*
If Aquinas is right that there is an essential human nature, then there really is a good for all humans that they should strive towards.	Aquinas may be making the mistake of assuming that all human beings have the same purposes; it may be possible that each of us has different purposes. Aquinas himself seems to allow this in his recognition that priests who are called to celibacy are exempt from the primary precept of reproduction.
While Aquinas supports *telos* with reason, divine command theory (which argues that right and wrong are based on the revealed commands of God) makes a similar point via revelation; the Bible reveals the 'plans and purposes that God has for human beings' (Jeremiah 29:13).	As shown above, existentialists dispute whether humans have any purpose except the ones they freely choose for themselves. If God does not exist, then it seems difficult to argue for objective human purpose.
	Similarly, the scientific theory of evolution seems to suggest that purpose is not a feature of the world, but is rather something that human beings project on to the natural world.
	The idea of *telos* entails that some things are natural to human beings and other things are unnatural.

Activities

Core

1 What does it mean to describe Sartre as an existentialist?
2 According to Sartre, what is the key difference between humans and man-made objects? Why does this matter?
3 What is divine command theory? How could it be used to address the question of whether right and wrong can be based on the idea of telos?

Stretch

4 Explain why atheism is essential to Sartre's ideas.
5 Look at the arguments for and against the significance of *telos*. Which argument is the strongest? Justify your answer.

Challenge

6 Find out more about the existentialism of thinkers such as Sartre. What impact does existentialism have on ethics?

1.4 Can the idea of double effect be used to justify actions?

Aim

Learn how natural law uses the idea of double effect and consider whether this is a good way of justifying actions.

Starter

Without looking at your notes or the previous pages of this textbook, write a paragraph explaining what natural law is and how it makes moral decisions. You should use the terms *telos*, synderesis, primary precepts and secondary precepts in your response.

Key term

Double effect The idea that if doing something good also produces a bad side-effect, it is still ethically permissible as the bad side-effect was not intended

Key quote

'Nothing hinders one act from having two effects, only one of which is intended ... Accordingly the act of self-defence may have two effects: one the saving of one's life; the other, the slaying of the aggressor ... Therefore this act, since one's intention is to save one's life, is not unlawful.'
(Aquinas, *Summa Theologica*)

Interior and exterior acts

To understand Aquinas' views on double effect, it is worth thinking about the distinction he makes between interior and exterior acts. For Aquinas, a good act must have a good motive (interior) as well as being a good action as viewed on the outside (exterior). This means that giving to charity solely because your teacher is watching is not truly a good thing. Likewise, stealing something because you feel sorry for someone in poverty is no better. The interior and the exterior act must both be good.

Interior (motive)	Exterior (action)	Aquinas' judgement
To impress the teacher	Giving to charity	Wrong – interior
To prevent starvation	Stealing bread	Wrong – exterior
To prevent starvation	Buying bread	Good

Aquinas on double effect – one action, two effects!

Life is not always straightforward and sometimes our actions have more than one effect. The doctrine of **double effect** covers some of these areas where an action may produce several effects: some good and some bad. For Aquinas, what matters is which effect is intended. To illustrate this he uses the example of self-defence, as seen in the quote. If you were attacked and your assailant was trying to do you serious harm, or perhaps even to kill you, your act of fighting off the attacker (one action) would have two effects. One effect would be the good effect of saving your own life. If, however, the attacker were killed in the struggle, this would be a bad effect, but Aquinas argues that you are not guilty of doing anything wrong. Linking back to interior and exterior acts, Aquinas argues that it is the intention that matters. If you intend the good effect, you are not held responsible for the secondary bad effect.

▲ Aquinas argues that if you kill someone in self-defence, it is not morally wrong

Applying double effect

How Aquinas and followers of natural law approach the idea of double effect can be seen in the examples below.

One action

Good effect (intended)

Bad effect (unintended)

▲ One action can have multiple very different effects

- **Abortion:** During pregnancy, a woman is told that her life is at risk if she continues with the pregnancy. Even if she and her doctors are devout Catholics who believe that the foetus is a life that is sacred, an operation to save the mother's life is permitted in spite of the consequences to the foetus. The doctor would be carrying out one action (an operation) with the intention of saving the mother's life (good effect) and the secondary effect of ending the life of the foetus (bad effect).

- **Euthanasia:** A doctor attempting to treat a seriously ill patient gives a large dose of a pain killer (action). This has the effect of relieving pain (good effect), which is the doctor's intention, but runs the risk of causing the death of the patient (bad effect). If the patient dies, the doctor has done nothing wrong according to natural law as this was an unintended, although not unforeseen, consequence of the action. Note that if this was a sadistic doctor who enjoyed shortening people's lives, then the answer would be completely different, despite the action being identical.

Analyse and evaluate

Double effect is a good way of justifying moral actions because:	*Double effect is not a good way of justifying moral actions because:*
Double effect allows some flexibility in an otherwise rigid moral decision-making procedure. An action that produces both good and bad effects is permitted provided the good one is intended.	The idea that a bad effect is permitted if it is unintended and secondary is difficult to judge. It is almost impossible to genuinely judge the intention of a person. It may appear that someone was acting in self-defence and that their attacker's death was an accident, but only they will ever know. Likewise, in the example of the doctor, there is no difference between the external actions of the one who wishes to relieve pain and the one who wants to kill.
It is a recognition of the complexity of real-life situations. Some absolutists such as Kant have no answer for situations where duties clash or competing goods cannot both be achieved. Double effect allows sufficient consequential thinking into natural law to solve some of these cases.	Similarly, it is difficult to know how far to press the idea of double effect and which areas it may cover. The use of contraception with the intention of saving life where HIV is spreading has proved a controversial area in the Roman Catholic Church. There may be other areas where double effect could be applied in order to save life or assist reproduction that may result in a slippery slope.

Activities

Core

1 Explain the idea of interior and exterior acts. Give an example of each.

2 Explain what is meant by the doctrine of double effect.

3 How does double effect apply in the case of euthanasia?

Stretch

4 Explain one of the key difficulties in using the idea of double effect.

5 Rank the arguments for and against double effect. Can you think of a counterargument to some of these points?

Challenge

6 Using your material from Question 5 above, write up an essay for a question that asks you to assess double effect.

1.5 Do human beings and all of creation really have an orientation towards the good?

Aim

Investigate whether natural law is correct to argue that all of creation, including human beings, is naturally inclined towards the good.

Starter

Consider this baby. Try to imagine what she would be like if she were left to her own devices without society's structure. Would she naturally become good? Would her behaviour be worse as a result, or would there be no effect?

Key terms

Apparent good An action which someone mistakenly thinks is a real good, but they have not reasoned correctly

Real good Actions which are actually good and consistent with the moral principles of natural law

Natural law and the good

Natural law thinkers, such as Aquinas, believe that the whole of creation, including humans, is ordered by God and is orientated towards the good. In order to understand this claim, it is worth looking at some of the Greek background to natural law.

Stoicism – the orientation of creation

Stoic philosophers, such as Zeno and Marcus Aurelius, viewed the world as an ordered place. God (or the gods) created it and left within it the '*logos*' or divine reason. This divine spark is within each of us, so the reasonable response of humans towards the ordered universe is to live an ordered life of virtuous actions. Right actions are those that we are able to rightly reason. The Roman orator Cicero famously suggested that the natural law is 'right reason in accordance with Nature'. He argues that these laws would continue to apply even if governments changed them; the laws would be broadly the same regardless of whether we were in Rome, Athens or elsewhere.

Aquinas – the orientation of human beings

Aquinas takes such insights, and Aristotle's view that the universe is drawn towards the prime mover, and fuses them with Christian thought. People are created in the image of God, the most significant aspect of this being '*ratio*' or the ability to reason. The synderesis principle suggests that we are directed by something within us to pursue good and avoid evil. Hence the ability to achieve the good is within each of us if we reason correctly.

This leads Aquinas to take an interesting view on moral mistakes. He follows Socrates in suggesting the seemingly odd view that no one ever deliberately does a wrong action. They make a reasoning error in pursuing an **apparent good** rather than a **real good**. If a man has an affair with someone despite being married, then Aquinas argues that he must at least on some level not truly think the act is wrong. He is committing the mistake of thinking that the pleasure he will gain is good; yet he is mistaken, as pleasure is an apparent good, not a real good.

Key quote

'to the natural law belongs everything to which a man is inclined according to his nature.'

'the theologian considers sin principally as an offence against God, whereas the moral philosopher considers it as being contrary to reason.'

(Aquinas, *Summa Theologica*)

Analyse and evaluate

There is an orientation towards the good because:	There is not an orientation towards the good because:
Stoicism and religious thinkers are able to appeal to the order present in creation – Paley's arguments on design (which you will cover in Philosophy) are examples of this type of approach.	An objection to the orientation of creation towards the good is to reject the teleological view of the universe that comes from the assumption of God or gods. Modern evolutionary views suggest that the universe and life on Earth are the result of random chance and do not have any orientation or goal in mind. Dawkins famously suggests that evolution is a 'blind watchmaker'.
Aquinas is right that we do want to live well and we naturally aim for goodness/happiness. Where we miss this, it is because we are unclear on what goodness is or differ about how to achieve it, but our aim is nevertheless the same.	The idea that humans have an orientation towards the good raises issues for some theologians. Augustine (AD356–430) argues that humans are fallen and affected by original sin. This extends to our ability to make good moral decisions and act upon them. Our will is divided. Aquinas recognises this point to some extent but places more emphasis on the image of God, which gives us 'ratio' or ability to reason.
Aquinas' ideas on natural law give a dignity to human beings and places faith in their ability to reason, *but* ... (See weakness 3.)	(From strength 3) ... as seen above, there is some suggestion that although it is commendable that Aquinas gives such priority to reason, he is being overly optimistic about what reason can achieve.
	Aquinas' view of real and apparent goods could be seen as a little naïve. It seems that some humans knowingly commit evil actions, and it is mistaken to suggest they are merely pursuing apparent goods. A glance at the day's news suggests that not all humans have a natural inclination towards the good.

Activities

Core

1 What is the difference between a real and an apparent good?
2 What is Aquinas' view on moral mistakes?
3 How might the idea of evolution oppose the view that there is an orientation towards the good?

Stretch

4 How do Stoics argue that the whole of creation, including all humans, has an orientation towards the good?

5 Write a conclusion to an essay asking you to consider whether humans do naturally aim for the good.

Challenge

6 Review the Philosophy topics of Arguments from Observation (design argument) and (if you are studying Developments in Christian Thought) Augustine's Teaching on Human Nature, and make notes on any synoptic links to this topic.

Wrap up

QUIZ

1 Whose idea of *telos* does Aquinas use in his theory of natural law?
2 What does the word *telos* mean?
3 List the five primary precepts.
4 Where might a Christian find the divine law?
5 According to Aquinas, why do people do bad things?
6 What is the name for an action that has two effects – one good and one bad – but where the good effect is intended?
7 Does natural law permit people to kill enemy soldiers in war?
8 Which is the highest tier of law according to Aquinas?
9 How might Sartre and existentialists criticise natural law?
10 Under what circumstance might natural law permit abortion?

GET READY

Summarising

1 Make a copy of the grid below. Without looking at your notes, aim to add four or five points in each box. You could further train your memory by trying to repeat the process after a couple of weeks.

Explain *telos* (Aristotle and Aquinas)	Explain primary and secondary precepts	Four tiers of law
Strengths of natural law	Issues around *telos*	Other issues with natural law
Explain and assess double effect	Real and apparent goods	My conclusion on natural law

2 Below are six words that can be used to describe ethical theories. What does each of the words mean? Which would you use to describe the theory of natural law? Explain your answer.

Religious, Secular, Absolutist, Relativist, Deontological, Teleological

Debate

3 'Is natural law a useful ethical theory?'

Discuss this in small groups and make a note of the points raised. Add them to your notes.

Going further

4   The ethical theory of proportionalism is a recent development of natural law by Bernard Hoose (1945–). This broadly accepts the principles of natural law, but draws on the principles of casuistry (applying the general principles to specific situations) to bring in more consequential thinking. It allows moral rules to be broken if there is a 'proportionate reason' to do so that would create less evil. The Catholic Church has opposed proportionalism as it fails to rule certain acts as intrinsically evil.

Find out more about the theory of proportionalism. Is it a development of natural law or a separate theory in its own right?

5   As studied in the context of the specification, natural law is most definitely a religious ethic. This need not be the case, however. The classical versions of natural law from the Stoics may have made some reference to the ordering of the world by the gods/nature, but this was more philosophical than religious. The order of nature was rational. This idea that natural law should be followed regardless of the existence of God is also found in the sixteenth century, where Hugo Grotius, a leading natural law thinker, argues that even if God does not exist, the rules of natural law can be established by reason.

Find out more about non-religious versions of natural law, such as the ideas of Stoicism or the views of Cicero.

6   For the brave: Look at the specification on page 1 and try to write a possible exam question. Bulletpoint (or write!) a model answer to your question and get your teacher to mark it.

CHECKLIST

I know, understand and can ...

☐ explain Aristotle's idea of *telos* and how Aquinas develops this concept

☐ explain Aquinas' views on the four levels of law and his ideas on primary and secondary precepts

☐ assess whether natural law enables good moral decisions to be made

☐ consider whether *telos* can be used to decide whether something is good or bad

☐ consider whether the universe has *telos* and whether humans have an orientation towards good

☐ assess whether the idea of double effect is helpful.

Get practising

Ask the expert

'I've noticed that my initial essay marks are quite low and my teacher has pointed out that although I do okay at AO1, I am struggling with the AO2. He used the word "assertion" – I'm not really sure what he is getting at. How do I improve my marks?' – Grace

The expert says

It is really important to work on AO2 at A level as 24 of the 40 marks are for assessment and evaluation. Notice those words 'assessment' and 'evaluation'. One common pitfall at A level is to put an argument forward, but not really develop or discuss it. It may be that you did reasonably well at GCSE with this style, but you may need a rethink at A level. As you give an argument, ask yourself – How good is this argument? Is there a possible counterargument or response that could be given? What judgement do I come to about the argument? If you are doing this, you are beginning to assess and consider arguments. This will lead to higher levels of response for AO2.

Grace's first attempt

One strength of natural law is that it relies on reasoning. Aquinas follows the idea of the Stoics that the world is an ordered place and that the moral rules can be worked out accordingly. The secondary precepts are worked out from the primary precepts and it is our ability to reason that is key to this theory.

The theory also gives religious believers an ethical theory they can use, as one of the primary precepts is to worship God and the divine law is one of the four tiers of law.

Grace has put forward two strengths of natural law, however the points are merely stated or asserted. She needs to establish why these would be strengths and then consider how strong a point each one is. It may be better to have one main point in the paragraph that is developed and argued through.

Grace's improved response

One possible advantage of natural law is its reliance on reasoning. It treats humans as mature persons who are able to be rational and to reflect on moral problems. This is shown in Aquinas' expectation that we use our own reason to move from the generic primary precepts to more specific secondary precepts. It is not clear that this is necessarily a strength, however. Firstly, some thinkers have worried that relying on reason means that the role of scripture is reduced (although natural law thinkers would argue there isn't necessarily disagreement between the two). A further challenge to the role of reason comes from the teaching of Augustine that humans are fallen and incapable of reasoning clearly; if Augustine is right about this, then this would mean that the use of reason is not really a key strength of natural law.

This is a better paragraph. There is depth here and Grace is considering the point rather than just stating it. This ought to lead to higher levels of AO2.

Situation ethics

An alternative religious ethic is given by American ethicist Joseph Fletcher, (1905–91) who argues that *agape* (love) is the only consideration that needs to be taken when making a moral decision.

Engage

At the end of the Second World War, the Russian army picked up a woman, Mrs Bergmeier, who was searching for food for her family. They detained her in a prisoner of war camp. She discovered that her husband and children were safe in Germany and trying to find her. The only way for her to leave the camp was to become pregnant. A camp guard offered to help her get pregnant! What should she do?

The true story of Mrs Bergmeier is discussed in Joseph Fletcher's book *Situation Ethics: The new morality*. She became pregnant via the guard and was returned to Germany. The family raised little Dietrich and loved him as much as their other children. Fletcher argues that Mrs Bergmeier's actions could be seen as the most loving thing to do in that situation.

The specification	
Content	*Key knowledge*
Fletcher's situation ethics, including: ● *agape*	● Origins of *agape* in the New Testament and its religious development in the writing of Fletcher
● the six propositions	● What they are and how they give rise to the theory of situation ethics and its approach to moral decision-making: 　1 Love is the only thing that is intrinsically good 　2 Love is the ruling norm in ethical decision-making and replaces all laws 　3 Love and justice are the same thing – justice is love that is distributed 　4 Love wills the neighbour's good regardless of whether the neighbour is liked or not 　5 Love is the goal or end of the act and that justifies any means to achieve that goal 　6 Love decides on each situation as it arises without a set of laws to guide it
● the four working principles	● What they are and how they are intended to be applied: 　1 Pragmatism: Based on experience rather than on theory 　2 Relativism: Based on making the absolute laws of Christian ethics relative 　3 Positivism: Begins with belief in the reality and importance of love 　4 Personalism: Persons, not laws or anything else, are at the centre of situation ethics
● conscience	● What conscience is and what it is not according to Fletcher, i.e. a verb not a noun; a term that describes attempts to make decisions creatively
Learners should have the opportunity to discuss issues raised by Fletcher's theory of situation ethics, including: ● whether or not situation ethics provides a helpful method of moral decision-making ● whether or not an ethical judgement about something being good, bad, right or wrong can be based on the extent to which, in any given situation, *agape* is best served ● whether Fletcher's understanding of *agape* is really religious or whether it means nothing more than wanting the best for the person involved in a given situation ● whether or not the rejection of absolute rules by situation ethics makes moral decision-making entirely individualistic and subjective.	

2.1 What are the key ideas of situation ethics?

Aim

Understand the key ideas of Fletcher's situation ethics.

Starter

In 1841, the ship *William Brown* struck an iceberg near Newfoundland and began to sink. In one of the lifeboats were seven crew and 32 passengers (twice what the lifeboat could hold without sinking). The male passengers were ordered into the sea. When they refused, they were thrown there. Fletcher speaks approvingly of this action, suggesting that 'it was bravely sinful, it was a good thing'. What do you think? Was this the most loving thing to do?

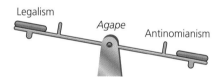

▲ Fletcher argues that *agape* is the midpoint between two unhelpful extremes

Key terms

Legalism Relying too heavily on laws or rules
Antinomianism Having no rules or laws at all

Love corrects two main errors

Fletcher sees situation ethics as the only sensible approach to ethics as it avoids the two unhelpful extremes in ethical thought.

- **Legalism** is an over-reliance on applying endless rigid rules. The Jewish law of the Old Testament has 613 separate rules. Jesus criticises this approach as it focuses on minor issues and misses the major ideas. He says that the Pharisees (teachers of the law) have a tendency to 'strain out a gnat but swallow a camel'. Fletcher argues, however, that later Christian thought has returned to a reliance on rules, particularly in the form of natural law.

- **Antinomianism** is literally a rejection of all moral laws (*nomos* means law in Greek). Twentieth-century philosophy has been affected by existentialism (see pages 6–7) and this has caused a rejection of moral laws and replaced them with the idea that the individual must make their own decisions.

Situation ethics argues that there is one moral rule – that we should do whatever is the most loving thing – and that this needs to be applied to each unique situation we face. Love is the absolute, but we should relativise it to the situation in front of us.

The four working principles – the foundations of situation ethics

Fletcher identifies four key philosophical principles that act almost as foundations to his theory.

1. **Pragmatism:** Pragmatism is a philosophical approach to truth based on the work of American philosophers such as William James and John Dewey. In order to count as true, something must work in practice. Likewise, Fletcher argues that theoretical solutions that don't lead to positive outcomes are not really solutions at all. The decision we make must be something that works and produces good outcomes.

2. **Relativism:** The right thing to do is dependent on the context. In ethics we should avoid terms like 'always' and 'never'. Although the principle of love always applies – love is the reason to act – the specifics of how love applies varies between situations.

3. **Positivism:** Unlike natural law, which argues that we can look into the world and effectively discover moral rules, situation ethics is based on a positivist approach to law. Laws are things that human beings create; we have to be active in bringing about love by the decisions we make.

4. **Personalism:** Unlike legalistic views, situation ethics is people-centred. Jesus placed people above rules – consider the case of the woman caught in adultery (John 8:1–11). The key to good ethics is to place the good of people at the centre, rather than obedience to rules.

The six propositions

Fletcher identifies six propositions that give rise to the theory of situation ethics and its approach to moral decision-making:

1 **'Only one thing is intrinsically good, namely love: nothing else at all':** Some things are extrinsically good – they help us to achieve a higher purpose, for example running may be good if we are late for the bus, but it is not good if we are indoors on a very slippery floor. Other things are good in themselves – they are intrinsically good. Only love is truly good in itself; Fletcher calls love the one regulative principle of Christian ethics.

2 **'The ruling norm of Christian decision is love, nothing else':** In the New Testament, Jesus consistently replaces the Old Testament laws with the principle of love, for example by healing someone (hence working) on the Sabbath. Where laws and love conflict, we must follow love. Fletcher reminds us that Jesus summed up the whole law as 'Love God' and 'Love your neighbour'.

3 **'Love and justice are the same, for justice is love distributed, nothing else':** Justice and love are not opposites as is often thought. Justice is Christian love applied rationally and in a calculated manner. Fletcher suggests that this is not a sentimental love, but is the calculation made by businessmen, generals or doctors in deciding who benefits the most.

4 **'Love wills the neighbour good, whether we like him or not':** Love is an attitude, not a feeling; the word *agape* used of love does not convey the warmth that the other Greek word *phileo* (friendship love) conveys. It is a selfless commitment or decision to treat others as best we can. It does not require anything in return. The Parable of the Good Samaritan illustrates that everyone is potentially our neighbour. Fletcher notes that Jesus' command to love even extends to loving our enemies (Matthew 5:43–48).

5 **'Only the end justifies the means, nothing else':** Fletcher argues that if our aim or end is love, then any means of achieving love is justified. It is whether the end is worthwhile that determines whether the action is worthwhile. Fletcher uses the example of Second World War resistance fighters who routinely lied and even killed members of their own side because of the importance of their cause.

6 **'Love's decisions are made situationally, not prescriptively':** Fletcher states that love decides 'there and then'. Knowing that we should love doesn't tell us what to do in a specific situation. We have to gather the facts, rather than decide the case before we know the facts. One particular issue is sexual ethics, where he argues that Christianity has become overly obsessed with rules, at the expense of deciding on a situational basis.

Activities

Core

1 What two extremes does situation ethics lie between?
2 Situation ethics is relativist. What does this mean?
3 According to Fletcher, how is the idea of loving someone related to the idea of liking them? Do you think he is right?

Stretch

4 Explain what Fletcher means when he says that love is an extrinsic good, rather than an intrinsic good.

5 Explain what Fletcher means when he describes situation ethics as pragmatic.

Challenge

6 Produce a poster to illustrate the six propositions of situation ethics. Try to think of some examples of your own.

2.2 Is situation ethics a helpful method of moral decision-making?

Aim

Investigate the strengths and weaknesses of situation ethics and draw conclusions about its helpfulness in terms of moral decision-making.

Starter

Without looking at your notes or the previous page, how many of Fletcher's four principles and six propositions can you remember?
You could do this on your own or work with a partner.

Meet the thinker

Biography: Joseph Fletcher was an ordained Episcopalian priest and professor of Christian ethics. His most famous work was his 1966 book *Situation Ethics: The new morality*. He was also president of the Euthanasia Society of America. Fletcher became an atheist in later life.

Key ideas: The ethical theory of situation ethics is most famously associated with Fletcher. He also wrote on the topics of abortion and euthanasia.

Appears in: Situation ethics, Euthanasia, Sexual ethics.

What exactly is *agape*?

Agape can be thought of as a summary of the ethics of Jesus. Whereas in English we only have one word for love, the Greek language has at least four:

- *Storge*: Love based on family connections
- *Philia*: Close friendship
- *Eros*: A sexual love (from which we get the word *erotic*)
- *Agape*: Charity, unconditional love

When Fletcher talks about love, he is referring to *agape*. The difference between the different types of love is explored by the Christian writer C.S. Lewis (1898–1963) in his 1960 book *The Four Loves*.

The Greek background of the word *agape* suggests a love for humankind. The word altruism helps to capture some of its meaning. Unlike *eros*, *agape* does not involve desire. For *agape*, the emotions involved lead to action. *Agape* is the greatest type of love because it exists regardless of circumstances. It is not natural to us and is a type of love that, according to Lewis, can only be practised with God's help.

Key quote

"'The most important one,' answered Jesus, 'is this: ... 'Love the Lord your God with all your heart and with all your soul and with all your mind and with all your strength.' The second is this: 'Love your neighbour as yourself.' There is no commandment greater than these.''"
(Mark 12:29–31)

Analyse and evaluate

Situation ethics may be seen as a helpful way of making moral decisions because:	Situation ethics may be seen as an unhelpful way of making moral decisions because:
A key attraction of situation ethics, as with all relativistic theories, is its flexibility. It is able to deal with exceptional situations, hence avoiding the legalism that some versions of natural law may lead us to. It enables people to keep the spirit of the law without being obsessed with the letter of the law.	Situation ethics faces the difficulty that, as a relativist theory, it is vague; the suggestion that we should do the most loving thing is not particularly specific or clear.
Situation ethics enables a decision to be made in each situation. Absolutist theories can struggle with difficult situations where there are two conflicting duties. Situation ethics enables us to choose the lesser of the two evils.	There are no moral boundaries. Everything could be permitted if the situation was extreme enough. This does not seem right. Some things – for example rape or genocide – are just inherently wrong and no circumstances could ever make them right.
Situation ethics is person-centred and as such seems closer to the teachings of Jesus, who consistently put people above rules.	Situation ethics as a teleological theory requires that we are able to make predictions about the outcome that our actions will produce. Yet we do not always know whether what we have done will produce the most loving outcome.
Love as a principle is hard to object to. If we love others, we will want the best for them. This seems more compassionate than some versions of utilitarianism, which just focus on pleasure and pain.	Similarly, it may be difficult to decide where a situation begins and ends. My decision to take a life to save others may be a good short-term solution, but may set in motion a chain of events and revenge that lasts for generations. How much am I responsible for at the moment of decision?
	Some critics have objected that situation ethics effectively becomes a Christian version of utilitarianism (see Chapter 4) that uses *agape* rather than pleasure and pain. Fletcher is aware of this point but does not necessarily see this as an objection to his theory.

Activities

Core

1 What are the two greatest commandments according to Jesus?
2 What does the term *agape* mean? (Try to use a word other than love!)
3 What is the key difference between *agape* and *eros*?

Stretch

4 What do you consider to be the strongest argument in support of situation ethics? Justify your answer.

5 What do you consider to be the strongest argument against situation ethics? Justify your answer.

Challenge

6 C.S. Lewis's *The Four Loves* is widely available online. Read Chapter 6, where Lewis discusses charity/*agape*.

2.3 Should ethical judgements really be based on *agape*?

Aim

Learn how Fletcher's situation ethics can be applied, and whether basing decisions on *agape* is an effective approach to ethics.

Starter

In what circumstances might a situation ethicist support abortion, euthanasia or breaking the law? Discuss this in small groups and note down the key points arising from your discussions.

Key quote

'Christian situationism is a method that proceeds ... from 1) its one and only law, *agape* (love), to 2) the *sophia* (wisdom) of the church and culture, containing many "general rules" of more or less reliability, to 3) the *kairos* (moment of decision, fullness of time) in which the responsible self in the situation decides whether the *sophia* can serve love there.'
(Joseph Fletcher, *Situation Ethics: The new morality*)

Applying love situationally

Fletcher sees situation ethics as a midpoint between the two errors of legalism and antinomianism (see page 16). For Fletcher, love is the ultimate law. We may have some general principles, which Fletcher calls *sophia* (the Greek word for wisdom), but love may mean that we break these.

Fletcher also places importance on the time and situation. He uses the word *kairos*, one of two Greek words for time, to refer to a significant time or season. In ethics, *kairos* is the 'moment of decision'. When applying love, we should consider the *sophia* and the *kairos,* and ask how love can be applied in that specific situation.

Case studies

One way that Fletcher vividly brings situation ethics to life in his book is through the use of case studies to show how the theory may be applied. We have already looked at the case of Mrs Bergmeier (page 15), and there are further applied cases on sexual ethics (page 130) and euthanasia/refusal of medical treatment (page 64) elsewhere in this book.

Case 1 – Acceptable abortion

In 1962, a young girl with schizophrenia was raped in a psychiatric hospital by a fellow patient. The victim's father charged the hospital with negligence and asked that an abortion be carried out to prevent the unwanted pregnancy. However, abortion was illegal in America at this time so the hospital staff refused, as abortion could only take place if the girl's life was in danger. Fletcher argues that this was the wrong decision and that a situationist approach would almost certainly support abortion in this case as the most loving thing.

Case 2 – Truman's Dilemma

During the Second World War, in August 1945, American aircraft dropped two atomic bombs on the Japanese cities of Hiroshima and Nagasaki. At least 150,000 people were killed and many more would go on to die from radiation burns or related conditions in the years that followed. Japan surrendered a few days later. The new US President, Harry Truman, had only learned of the technology that was available a few months previously, on his inauguration. Truman's inner circle of scientists and military advisers was split on whether it was right to use the atomic bomb to bring the war in Japan to an end. Several advisers pointed out that Japanese leaders were blind to the possibility of defeat and that 'honour' meant they were likely to continue fighting for years, leading to the possible loss of millions of lives. Others felt that a demonstration on a nearby uninhabited island would be a better strategy. It was left to Truman to make the final decision.

Analyse and evaluate

Ethical judgements should be based on agape because:	Ethical judgements should not be based on agape because:
For a religious thinker, *agape* is an excellent principle and, according to Jesus, sums up the most important commandments.	The concept of love represented by *agape* can be interpreted in various ways. It may for some conjure up charity and compassion, but for others represent a dispassionate wanting of good for others. As such, both the concept and the application to individual situations can produce different results.
The principle of *agape* is useful in helping us know when to accept the general rules (*sophia*) and when to break them. It is flexible to different situations.	One difficulty with *agape* and the idea of situation ethics in general is that it seems set up to deal with exceptional or difficult cases. But lawyers and philosophers often argue that hard cases make bad laws. *Agape* may be the right approach at times, but most cases require us to follow the conventional rules.
Agape is a relativist principle but, unlike the pleasure principle of utilitarianism, it does not seem as easy to manipulate. For instance, it is harder to argue that murder or racism can be a loving act even though in extreme circumstances this may bring pleasure to an evil majority.	There may be better principles upon which to base ethics. These may involve pleasure, duty or purpose according to other ethical theories in the specification. Additionally, a religious believer may argue that God directly reveals commands and that a stress on *agape* may lead a believer away from the revelation.

Activities

Core

1   What does Fletcher mean by the terms *sophia* and *kairos*?
2   Look at the key quote on page 20. Try to rewrite it in your own words.
3   Look at the points given in the table on page 19. Would any of these points also apply to a discussion on *agape*? Add them to your notes, explaining how they apply.

Stretch

4   Choose one of the case studies on the previous page. Which decision would be the most loving thing? Could the opposite view also be argued?

5   Write a conclusion to an essay asking whether ethical judgements should be based on *agape*. You can use the points above or your own ideas.

Challenge

6   Read the Appendix of Fletcher's book *Situation Ethics*. It contains a number of case studies. Add one of them to your notes, showing how you might use it in an essay.

2.4 Is situation ethics really a religious ethic?

Agape in Christian tradition

Aim

Investigate the extent to which situation ethics can be understood as a religious, rather than a secular, theory of ethics.

Starter

Working in pairs, what are the similarities and differences between situation ethics and natural law?

Use the words absolutist, relativist, deontological, teleological, religious and secular to stimulate your thoughts. Look back at the Introduction (pages ix–x) to remind yourself of these terms if you need to.

Christianity emerged from Judaism in the first century CE. Judaism at that time had many debates about how far to take interpretation of the law. Some argued that each of the 613 laws was equally important and should be kept, whereas others argued for a simpler interpretation. Just prior to the time of Jesus, the Rabbi Hillel famously said, 'That which is hateful to you, do not do to your neighbour. That is the whole Torah; the rest is commentary.' Hence the idea was established in many people's minds that loving God and loving one's neighbour were the two most important commandments.

Jesus offers a radical version of this. He summarises the law as the requirement to love God and love your neighbour. He breaks Sabbath laws to heal people, thus bringing about a more loving outcome. He allows his disciples to pick and eat grain in a field, again breaking Sabbath law. The story of the Good Samaritan reinforces the idea of love for one's neighbor, regardless of whether we like them or not. Fletcher cites a number of these examples to show the danger of legalism and to argue that Jesus' ethics were based on *agape*.

As seen in the key quotes below, elsewhere in the New Testament Paul argues that the greatest of the virtues is love, and John's writings are littered with references to the importance of love.

Key quotes

'If I give all I possess to the poor and give over my body to hardship that I may boast, but do not have love, I gain nothing … and now these three remain: faith, hope and love. But the greatest of these is love.'
(Paul in 1 Corinthians 13:3, 13)

'Anyone who claims to be in the light but hates a brother or sister is still in the darkness. Anyone who loves their brother and sister lives in the light and there is nothing in them to make them stumble.'
(1 John 2:9–10)

Key quote

'There is only one ultimate and invariable duty, and its formula is "Thou shalt love thy neighbour as thyself". How to do this is another question, but this is the whole of moral duty.'
(Archbishop William Temple, *Mens Creatix*)

In the fourth century, Augustine famously suggested that people should 'love God and do what they will', as if they truly love God they will be guided to do the right thing. Likewise, Aquinas' double effect and the twentieth-century theory of proportionalism (see page 62) might bring more flexibility in Christian ethical thinking than is generally realised. In the early twentieth century, Archbishop William Temple argued that love is the main duty that Christians have. There are also ideas of love in the ethics of Bonhoeffer, whose faith led him to plot against Hitler. Thus, the idea that love is key to Christian ethics is not new. Fletcher is being more radical, however, in suggesting that love is the *only* principle needed in Christian ethics.

Analyse and evaluate

Situation ethics is to be seen as a religious ethical theory because:	Situation ethics should not really be seen as a religious ethical theory because:
The ethic is very clearly located in the words of Jesus, who, when asked to sum up the whole of the Jewish Law, suggested that only two commands are needed: 'Love God' and 'Love your neighbour as yourself'.	Situation ethics has been rejected by the established Church. It was condemned at the time of Fletcher's writing by Pope Pius XII. It was in clear opposition to natural law on a number of key issues.
Jesus' attitudes to the Pharisees (the religious scholars) in the New Testament shows a clear opposition to the legalism of his day. A good religious ethic does not have to be based on hard-and-fast rules.	It can be argued that Fletcher's reading of the words of Jesus is highly selective. Jesus quite clearly condemns divorce and adultery, and speaks about hell far more than he speaks about heaven.
The idea that love is the key evidence of genuine religious faith is found in the words of Jesus: 'By this everyone will know that you are my disciples, if you have love for one another' (John 13:34–35) and in the teachings of Augustine.	Jesus tells his disciples that if they love him they are to obey his commandments – that implies that there are commandments other than love.
	Fletcher's interpretation of *agape* as an unconditional wishing the best for our neighbour is not explicitly Christian. In reality, there is little difference between situation ethics and act utilitarianism. Fletcher is not overly worried by this, however, and at one point in his book suggests that situation ethics is basically a Christian utilitarianism.

Activities

Core

1   In what ways does Jesus show that he is not a legalist?
2   Apart from the teachings of Jesus, what other evidence is there that love is important in Christian ethics?
3   Which of Fletcher's propositions is illustrated by the Parable of the Good Samaritan (Luke 10:25–37)?

Stretch

4   Why might a supporter of natural law find it difficult to support situation ethics? What are the key differences?

5   To what extent was Jesus a situation ethicist? Look at the material on this page and in other topics you have studied. Write 2–3 paragraphs justifying your views.

Challenge

6   Find out more about the tradition of love in Christian ethics by reading about the ethical ideas of Augustine, Niebuhr, Temple or Bonhoeffer.

2.5 Is situation ethics too individualistic and subjective?

Aim

Understand Fletcher's views on the conscience and consider whether situation ethics may be too individualistic and subjective to provide good moral decisions.

Starter

Look at the cartoon. What would be the most loving thing to do? What else would the officer need to know? Would other people in the situation make a different decision? Why?

Key quote

'It is an individual and subjective appeal to the concrete circumstances of actions to justify decisions in opposition to the Natural Law or God's revealed will.' Pope Pius XII, criticising situation ethics

Key term

Subjective The idea in ethics that right and wrong depend on the point of view of the individual rather than being decided externally

▲ A man is running for the train. The police officer believes he looks similar to the description of a terrorist that they have received a tip-off about

The role of the individual

Fletcher rejects both legalism and antinomianism in favour of the one overriding ethical principle of *agape*, that in each situation we are required to do whatever brings about the most loving outcome. In doing so, he places emphasis on the individual to make the decision. There is no need to consult external authorities; the person in the situation has the moment of decision (he uses the word *kairos* – see page 20). This may lead to the concern that the theory becomes very **subjective**, as what is most loving is a matter of personal opinion.

Conscience

Fletcher's remarks on conscience shed some light on the idea of individualism at the heart of this theory. Fletcher argues that traditional understandings of the conscience are mistaken. Conscience is often seen as a thing – a noun. This may be either the voice of God within us according to Catholic thinker J.H. Newman (1801–90), or an inbuilt reasoning tool in the thinking of Aquinas.

Yet conscience is not a thing that we possess, it is rather an activity that we do. It is a function not a faculty. Conscience is a verb not a noun and it refers to the process of deciding. It is best understood as something that looks forward in terms of prospective decision-making rather than something that retrospectively passes judgement on our actions after the event. Fletcher cites Paul's reference to the conscience in the New Testament in support of this and states that conscience is a director (before and during the event) not a reviewer (after the event).

For Fletcher, every individual and situation is unique. Hence the Christian, after prayerful consideration, has to decide how to apply love. Any moral principles they have must be kept in check – these principles are guides and advisers but do not have the final word. This process of thoughtful decision-making is the process of 'conscience-ing'.

Analyse and evaluate

It can be argued that situation ethics is not too individualistic and subjective because:	It can be argued that situation ethics is too individualistic and subjective because:
Rather than relying on external authorities, situation ethics gives responsibility and autonomy in moral decision-making. Thus situation ethics treats individuals as adults.	The emphasis on individual decision-making means that this could never be an ethic that could be applied in a society, as views of love differ.
Situations and contexts do differ greatly and it is important that flexibility is retained. Situation ethics recognises that what is right for one person in a specific situation may not suit other people who are faced with a slightly different situation.	Other thinkers who have used love as the basis of decision-making have continued to recognise the importance of community for ethical decision-making. For instance, Bonhoeffer's community at Finkenwalde made decisions based on communal Bible reading, prayer and conversation. They recognised the importance of other people in discerning the right course of action.
	Situation ethics may be overly optimistic about our capacity to reason clearly and reach moral decisions. Psychologists refer to the phenomenon of cognitive dissonance, which makes it difficult for us to accept evidence that goes against a deeply held belief. Theologians such as Augustine and Barth would also be cautious about our ability to reach good decisions, as humans are fallen creatures and this affects our reasoning.
	Fletcher's view on conscience as being a key process in decision-making is a little vague in terms of detail. In criticising other views he arguably misinterprets Aquinas, whose views on conscience may be closer to Fletcher's than he realises.
You may also wish to look at the strengths and weaknesses of situation ethics suggested elsewhere in this chapter and consider which points also apply here.	

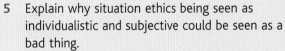

Activities

Core

1   What does it mean to say that situation ethics is an individualistic theory of decision-making?
2   What does Fletcher mean by suggesting that conscience is a verb not a noun?
3   Why might a belief in the Fall and Original Sin be a problem for Fletcher?

Stretch

4   Explain why situation ethics being seen as individualistic and subjective could be seen as a good thing.

5   Explain why situation ethics being seen as individualistic and subjective could be seen as a bad thing.

Challenge

6   Research the idea of cognitive dissonance. Why might this phenomenon pose a problem for the method of decision-making that Fletcher proposes?

Wrap up

QUIZ

1 What are the four different Greek words for love?

2 What does Jesus say are the two most important commandments?

3 Fletcher sees a _____ as the midpoint between the extremes of _____ and _____ .

4 What philosophical position on truth held by James and Dewey influences Fletcher?

5 What four working principles underpin Fletcher's theory?

6 How does Fletcher address the apparent difference between love and justice?

7 How important is it to Fletcher that we like other people?

8 How does Fletcher answer the objection that situation ethics is a Christian utilitarianism?

9 Is situation ethics a deontological or teleological theory of ethics?

10 How can Fletcher's use of the Bible be criticised?

 Tip

If you are studying Developments in Christian Thought, you will come across the idea that ethical decisions should be based entirely on love in the Christian moral principles topic.

There are a number of opportunities if you are studying Developments in Christian Thought to make links in this topic to your study of Augustine and human nature as well as Bonhoeffer.

GET READY

Summarising

1 Copy and complete the table below.

Key term	Explanation/definition
Agape	
	An over-reliance on rules that some religious ethical systems suffer from
Pragmatism	
	The idea that it is more important to focus on people than on rules
Antinomianism	
	The idea that the right thing to do is dependent upon the context
Positivism	

Applying

2 Make a concept map for situation ethics on paper or use an online concept-mapping tool such as Coggle. You should ensure that you focus on both AO1 and AO2. A suggested outline is shown below, but you are free to use your own branches.

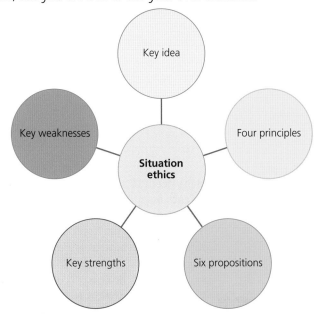

3 AO2 focus: Make a list of the strengths of situation ethics. Score each one out of 10 according to how persuasive you think it is. Repeat the process with the weaknesses. You could discuss your answers to this task with a friend and try to justify your views where they differ.

4 Developing a conclusion: Using your answers to Question 3, evaluate some of the key points, perhaps giving a counterargument. Use these to write a conclusion to an essay evaluating situation ethics.

 Tip

A common issue when candidates write about situation ethics is that they don't fully understand *agape*. This leads to essays where love is equated to being nice to others or having warm feelings towards them. This fails to distinguish *agape* from romantic or family love similar to that we may have seen on films! *Agape* is an unconditional love that leads to action regardless of whether it is felt or not.

Debate

5 'The outcome achieved is more important than whether moral rules are followed.'

Use your knowledge of natural law and situation ethics to discuss this in pairs before using your ideas as a basis for a class debate.

CHECKLIST

I know, understand and can ...

- ☐ explain Fletcher's understanding of *agape*
- ☐ explain Fletcher's six propositions that he uses to explain situation ethics
- ☐ explain Fletcher's four working principles: positivism, relativism, positivism, and personalism
- ☐ explain Fletcher's understanding of conscience as a verb not a noun
- ☐ assess whether situation ethics is a useful means of making moral decisions
- ☐ consider whether ethical judgements can be based on the concept of *agape*
- ☐ assess the extent to which Fletcher's theory of *agape* is genuinely a religious theory
- ☐ consider the criticism that situation ethics is individualistic and subjective.

Get practising

Ask the expert

'I am struggling to get more than a grade C or D or my essays. I get good marks for knowledge and understanding, but struggle to argue. My teacher has suggested that I try to think about AO2 more in the planning stage. I'm not sure what this might look like.' – Harry

Harry's essay plan

P1 – Introduction

P2 – Explain *agape* – link to legalism and antinomianism

P3 – Explain four principles

P4 – Explain six propositions – use examples

P5 – Strengths of situation ethics: flexible, people-centred, Jesus

P6 – Weaknesses of situation ethics: love is vague, no boundaries, basically utilitarian

P7 – Conclusion

Harry needs to bear in mind that 24 of the 40 marks on each essay are for AO2 – analysis and evaluation. Only two or possibly three of his seven paragraphs are AO2 paragraphs. There is also the risk in covering three strengths or weaknesses in one paragraph that points will be stated rather than fully discussed. This will make it difficult to access the higher levels of the AO2 mark scheme. Naqeeb's essay plan below avoids this difficulty.

Naqeeb's essay plan

P1 – Intro – what is SE – SE not good method of decision-making

P2 – SE is flexible to situations, e.g. lying to save lives, BUT lack of moral boundaries SO flexibility not a clear strength

P3 – SE focuses on people – principle of personalism – Mrs Bergmeier case – BUT love is subjective – however some merit in point

P4 – SE too vague – different interpretations of *agape*, e.g. would it be right to kill the terrorist?

P5 – SE individualistic – Fletcher on conscience – we are left to judge *agape* ourselves – BUT this needn't be the case – Bonhoeffer's community discussed/prayed together – BUT issue of individualism remains

P6 – SE too close to utilitarianism – Fletcher doesn't see this as weakness BUT problem of predicting future and lack of boundaries that util. has remains – so issue stands

P7 – Conclusion – respect for persons useful but otherwise weaknesses remain

CHAPTER 3

Kantian ethics

Big picture

A third approach to ethics is the idea that what makes an action right or wrong is whether it fulfils our duties. Kant argues that all human beings have duties, not just those of us with certain jobs. There are certain actions that are good and we should do them regardless of our feelings and regardless of the outcome.

Engage

▲ The health secretary has warned reality TV shows they have a **duty of care** for contestants following the death of *Love Island* star Mike Thalassitis

▲ The New York Firefighters who went towards the fires and up the staircases during 9/11 insist "we were just doing our **duty**"

▲ Dr Conrad Murray is sentenced for his part in the death of the singer Michael Jackson. The judge claimed he had failed in his **duty** as a doctor

What do we learn about the idea of duty from these three examples? What types of people might have duties? What are those duties?

We accept that certain professions involve duties. Your teacher has a duty to teach the correct material. A police officer has a duty to intervene if they see a crime being committed. A doctor has a duty to save life. What duties do you think that all people have in terms of how they treat others?

The specification	
Content	*Key knowledge*

Kantian ethics, including:
• duty
 	
• the hypothetical imperative
 	
• the categorical imperative and its three formulations
 	
• the three postulates
	• Origins of the concept of duty (acting morally according to the good regardless of consequences) in deontological and absolutist approaches to ethics
	• What it is (a command to act to achieve a desired result) and why it is not the imperative of morality
	• What it is (a command to act that is good in itself regardless of consequences) and why it is the imperative of morality based on:
	  1 Formula of the law of nature (whereby a maxim can be established as a universal law)
	  2 Formula of the end in itself (whereby people are treated as ends in themselves and not means to an end)
	  3 Formula of the kingdom of ends (whereby a society of rationality is established in which people treat each other as ends and not means)
	• What they are and why in obeying a moral command they are being accepted:
	  1 Freedom 2 Immortality 3 God

Learners should have the opportunity to discuss issues raised by Kant's approach to ethics, including:
• whether or not Kantian ethics provides a helpful method of moral decision-making
• whether or not an ethical judgement about something being good, bad, right or wrong can be based on the extent to which duty is best served
• whether or not Kantian ethics is too abstract to be applicable to practical moral decision-making
• whether or not Kantian ethics is so reliant on reason that it unduly rejects the importance of other factors, such as sympathy, empathy and love, in moral decision-making.

3.1 What are the key ideas of Kantian ethics?

Aim

Understand the key ideas of Kantian ethics.

Meet the thinker

▲ Immanuel Kant (1724–1804)

Biography and key ideas:
Immanuel Kant was born in Konigsberg (now Kaliningrad) in the east of Prussia. His writings include *The Critique of Pure Reason, The Critique of Practical Reason*, and *The Groundwork of the Metaphysics of Morals*. Kant's epistemology (theory of knowledge) argued that the mind organises our experience so that there is phenomena (how the world appears) and noumena (how the world really is). Kant uses this to argue that it is impossible to prove God's existence but that moral truths are somehow built into the world.

Appears in: Sexual ethics and Business ethics, as well as Philosophy of Religion (Kant's criticism of the ontological argument in arguments using reason).

Kantian ethics – good will and duty

> ### Key term
>
> **Duty** Acting morally according to good regardless of the consequences

When people are asked what is good, they may give lots of different answers. For instance, making other people happy may be good, but it wouldn't be good if you were making people happy by torturing others. Courage is generally good, but there are situations where you can courageously do the wrong thing. Kant says that the only thing that is good at all times is a 'good will'. This means having a good intention – an intention to do our **duty**.

Our actions might be motivated by lots of different things. Kant rules out two false intentions. Firstly, we should not base our views of right and wrong on consequences as these are not within our control. Secondly, we should not base our decisions on our inclinations (what we want to do), as our emotions change on a regular basis. One day we will feel like doing the right thing, the next day we won't. Kant argues that the thing that does matter is that we do our duty; the thing that we logically work out is the right thing to do. We should do our duty just because it is our duty, not for any reward.

Working out what my duty is – categorical and hypothetical imperatives

> ### Key term
>
> **Maxim** The rule that we are following when we perform an action

Kant believes that it is possible to work out what our duty is by establishing what sort of command (or imperative) lies behind it. When we carry out an action, Kant believes we have a rule or **maxim** in mind. We need to establish whether it is a hypothetical imperative or a categorical imperative. **Hypothetical imperatives** are 'if …' commands. Your personal trainer might say 'Don't eat more cake', but what is actually meant is 'Don't eat more cake, *if* you want to lose weight'. Other commands are categorical – there is no 'if' about them, they are absolute. 'Do not kill' might be one such command. It is our duty to act on anything that is a **categorical imperative**.

> ### Key terms
>
> **Hypothetical imperative** A command that is followed to achieve a desired result
>
> **Categorical imperative** A command that is good in itself regardless of consequences

Finding the categorical imperative

Kant suggests that there are three different tests that can be applied to a maxim in order to see if it is a categorical imperative.

1 **Formula of the law of nature (universal law):** If we are considering an action, we should ask ourselves, 'Would it be logical for this action to be universalised?' (i.e. would it make sense if everyone did this?). For example, it would not make sense to universalise stealing. Stealing is taking someone else's property. If we were to universalise stealing, then no one would really own anything, leading to an illogical conclusion: if everyone were always stealing, there would be no stealing.

2 **Persons as ends:** A second test of our maxim is how it treats people. Kant believes that we should treat people as an end in themselves; as free rational beings who deserve dignity and respect. We should not treat them as a means to an end, using them to achieve some sort of purpose. We can use objects in this way but we should not use people.

3 **Kingdom of ends:** The final test is almost a combination of the first two. Kant asks us to imagine we are part of the law-making group in an imaginary country where everyone always treats others as an end. Kant suggests that a categorical imperative is an imperative that could be permitted in such a place.

One common objection to Kant's second formulation is that we can't avoid treating others as a means to an end. When we buy things in a shop, are we not using the shopkeeper? When we come to college, are we using our teacher as a means to a good grade? Kant would not think so. The word 'solely' often gets missed. We are not to treat others *solely* as a means to an end. Hopefully, in your interactions with shop assistants, teachers and the like you are showing that you do also consider them to be persons!

Criticising Kant: morality is a system of hypothetical imperatives

Moral philosopher Philippa Foot (1920–2010) challenges Kant's view that morality should be based on a series of categorical imperatives. Foot's key interest is to answer the question of why we should be moral (which also interested Plato). In her 1995 essay 'Morality as a System of Hypothetical Imperatives', Foot argues that what is missing from Kant's account is an adequate explanation of our motives and desires. Only hypothetical imperatives give us a reason to act, for example 'If you want to get an A you should study more often.' We have a clear reason to act in a certain way. In Kant's categorical imperatives, we are just told that we must do a certain thing; there is no account of motives.

Foot is influenced by the virtue ethics of Aristotle and thinks that this may help with the issue of motivation. Many of the virtues and good character traits of human action are things that we must freely choose; they are contingent. It is hoped that these virtues are things we desire and that they motivate us to action – but they may not. Everything about morality is hypothetical. In a reinterpretation of one of Kant's remarks, Foot suggests that we should not be conscripts forced to be virtuous, but rather volunteers.

Activities

Core

1 Why are inclinations and consequences not a good guide as to what we should do?
2 What are the main differences between hypothetical and categorical imperatives?
3 What three tests can be applied to find the categorical imperative?

Stretch

4 Sort the following imperatives into two columns: hypothetical and categorical:
Eat less cake; do not kill; tell the truth; take RS at A level; go to the gym more; be faithful to your partner; do not steal; do your homework.

Try devising some hypothetical and categorical imperatives of your own to add to the list.
5 Write a paragraph explaining Kant. You should aim to do this in 100 words or fewer.

Challenge

6 Kant has two slightly different formulations of the idea of universal law: contradiction in conception and contradiction in will. Find out about the difference between these two things.

3.2 Does Kantian ethics provide a helpful way of making moral decisions?

 Aim

Understand the main strengths and weaknesses of Kantian ethics.

 Starter

Kant's ethics involve ideas such as duty, categorical imperative, universal law and person as ends. Take turns at trying to explain these concepts to each other without looking at your notes.

Kant on good will

Kant argues that the only thing that is truly and intrinsically good is a 'good will'. For all other things – e.g. pleasure, courage, love – there would be a 'qualification'. There would be a circumstance that we could think of where this was not good. This is not true of good will; this is always good.

Kant argues that good will is good purely because of the intention and desire to do the right thing. He explains that even if, despite our best efforts, our willing achieves nothing, this would not matter. For Kant, intentions and actions matter more than consequences.

 Key quote

'Nothing can possibly be conceived in the world, or even out of it, which can be called good, without qualification, except a good will.'

'A good will is good not because of what it effects, or accomplishes, not because of its fitness to attain some intended end, but good just by its willing ..., if despite its greatest striving it should still accomplish nothing, and only the good will were to remain then, like a jewel, it would still shine by itself, as something that has full worth in itself.'

(Immanuel Kant, *Groundwork of the Metaphysics of Morals*)

Kant on formulations of the categorical imperative

For Kant, these key quotes show the two main ways that we can establish what our duty is. It is wrong for us to carry out an action that we couldn't logically desire all people do. In addition, we are required to consider persons as we act. This includes valuing and respecting ourselves just as we should do others.

 Key quote

'Act only according to that maxim by which you can at the same time will that it should become a universal law.'

'Act in such a way that you treat humanity, whether in your own person or in the person of any other, never merely as a means to an end, but always at the same time as an end.'

(Immanuel Kant, *Groundwork of the Metaphysics of Morals*)

Analyse and evaluate

Kantian ethics is helpful regarding our duty to ourselves as well as to others because:	*Kantian ethics is not helpful regarding our duty to ourselves as well as to others because:*
Duty as an idea is better than depending on our inclinations. Our inclinations (what we want to do or feel like doing) are led by our emotions, which change. We are also less prone to personal bias if duty is our key principle.	While there is clarity about Kant's rules, as with any absolutist ethical system there is inflexibility to the situation. For instance, Kant establishes that lying is morally wrong. He thinks it is morally wrong even to lie to a murderer seeking his next victim. The idea that you must still do your duty and that it is the potential murderer whose actions are immoral will not be of much comfort to the victim!
Similarly, Kant's ethics are rational. Kant gives human beings the responsibility for making decisions and he believes that humanity's ability to reason and work things out will enable us to reach the right answers.	Similarly, the outcome of a situation is ignored. Although the outcome is not always within our control, the outcome of our actions is often foreseeable and predictable. To choose to do something that obeys a moral rule but will almost certainly lead to increased misery or suffering seems like the wrong decision.
Kant is right that consequences can't be predicted. Systems such as situation ethics and utilitarianism require us to make predictions about the future result of our actions. We cannot be held responsible for things that are not within our control.	Kant gives no clear guidance on what to do when duties clash. In the example of the murderer above, we can universalise telling the truth and we can also universalise trying to save a life. It would appear that both of these could be categorical imperatives. We cannot do both and Kant gives us no way of deciding between conflicting duties.
Kant's principle of universal law is a useful rule. It has similarities with the principle that is found in all the main religious faiths of not doing things to others that you would not wish to be done to you.	Kant's ethics is a good theoretical solution to many moral issues; his kingdom of ends shows his aim to make moral rules for an ideal world. Ethics is about how the world ought to be. This ignores reality, however. Life is complicated and in the real world Kant's solutions and ideas can often appear impractical.
Kant's ethics values persons. In addition to respecting their rationality, his principle of treating persons as ends is helpful in practical ethics and, in contrast to the utilitarians, ensures that every human being is significant.	The principle of universal law does not necessarily show us our moral duties. Non-moral maxims can logically be universalised, for example 'Everyone should sing the national anthem each Wednesday morning' could be universalised, but it is not clear that this is a real moral duty! Similarly, just because I cannot universalise something doesn't mean it is immoral. I cannot universalise the eating of nuts as some people have allergies, but that does not suggest that I should not eat nuts.
Modern views of justice and rights owe much to Kantian ethics, particularly the focus on persons.	
Kant's ethics can be seen as secular. The principles can be applied by people of all faiths and people of no faith.	

Activities

Core

1 According to Kant, what is the only thing that is truly good?
2 How does Kant suggest that we treat persons?
3 What is the problem of conflicting duties?

Stretch

4 Look at the points in the table arguing that Kant's ethics is helpful. Which two points are the strongest? Justify your answer.

5 Look at the points in the table arguing that Kant's ethics is not helpful. Which two points are the strongest? Justify your answer.

Challenge

6 Kant argues that there are moral absolutes – for example that lying or killing is always wrong. Write a speech for a debate on whether Kant is right. Use the points in the table above as a stimulus.

3.3 Does what is right and wrong depend on duty?

Aim

Learn about the idea of duty as applied in Kantian ethics.

Starter

Read the dialogue below. What are your initial thoughts on whether ethics can be motivated by duty?

Vic: I really don't like that new topic about Kant's ethics.

Rick: How come, my friend?

Vic: Well, if I wanted to live my life by duty I would have joined the police service or gone into nursing. Duty is just not something that ordinary people have.

Rick: I'm not sure Kant would agree with you there. You might not have duties written into your contract at Burgerz4U, but surely you owe your employer a duty to work hard while you are there.

Vic: Maybe, but that leads me to another worry I have. My duty at work is to do everything that my manager tells me. If we all start just doing what people in charge tell us then I worry that we could end up doing some pretty awful stuff. It seems wrong to say that we should just follow orders.

Rick: I'm not sure duty is as simple as that. Kant thinks that duty is something you need to work out.

Vic: Wouldn't that make duty rather vague? Suppose you work out that it is wrong to steal a sandwich to feed the hungry and I work out that it would be morally good. Which of us is right?

Rick: But the key point in favour of duty is that it is rational; it would not be possible for us to come to different conclusions if we were thinking clearly.

Vic: I'm not sure that's right. I think I have a slightly different example that may help. Suppose you are asked by a murderer if you know where your friend is hiding. Would you not at that time have one duty to tell the truth and another duty to save a life? Could you not have two opposite duties?

Rick: Reminds me of the time you hid from the French teacher over that missing homework. But we digress. I think you make a fair point here. I'm not sure how to answer you, but I do think on balance that duty is a good motivator. Too often we act based on whether we feel like doing something and we know that our emotions change, so duty for me seems better.

Vic: But what if you do your duty knowing that there will be negative consequences? Surely that is also important.

Rick: This is about me telling the French teacher you were in the cupboard, isn't it?

Going further: perfect and imperfect duties

Kant suggests that there are two types of duties: perfect duties and imperfect duties. A perfect duty is one where our maxim cannot be universalised because a logical contradiction would occur if we were to do so. The example in the key quote in the margin of page 35 covers the perfect duty of keeping promises. If we were to make a false promise, we promise something but have no intention of carrying out the promise, this is something that logically cannot be universalised as the whole concept of promising relies on the idea that people are telling the truth when they

Key quote

'Suppose, however, that he resolves to do so [make a false promise], then the maxim of his action would be expressed thus: When I think myself in want of money, I will borrow money and promise to repay it, although I know that I never can do so. ... but the question now is, Is it right? ... How would it be if my maxim were a universal law? Then I see at once that it could never hold as a universal law of nature, but would necessarily contradict itself.'

(Immanuel Kant, *Groundwork of the Metaphysics of Morals*)

make promises. If everyone were to be lying when making promises, then the very idea of promises is destroyed.

Other duties do not create a logical contradiction but they do present us with a situation that no rational person could desire or will. These are known as imperfect duties. In the example below we could conceive of a world where people didn't help others in need – it is not illogical in the way that a false promise is illogical – but a rational person could not sincerely desire or will to be part of such a world.

Key quote

'[A man], who is in prosperity, while he sees that others have to contend with great wretchedness and that he could help them, thinks: What concern is it of mine? ... I do not wish to contribute anything to his welfare or to his assistance in distress! Now no doubt, if such a mode of thinking were a universal law, the human race might very well subsist, ... But it is impossible to will that such a principle should have the universal validity of a law of nature. For a will which resolved this would contradict itself ... he would deprive himself of all hope of the aid he desires [if he were in that situation].'

(Immanuel Kant, *Groundwork of the Metaphysics of Morals*)

Analyse and evaluate

Right and wrong does depend on duty because:	*Right and wrong does not depend on duty because:*
Duty is rational and as such is not subject to our changing emotions or circumstances.	The concept of duties is useful in public sector employment but does not seem to apply to every area of life.
The concept of duty rightly involves giving to each person the things that we owe in terms of how we treat them. Thus it allows us to respect persons.	There is a danger of conflating duty with obedience to authority.
	There are often issues with conflicting duties, where we cannot fulfil both of the good actions that seem to be required.

Activities

Core

1   What misunderstandings are there in the dialogue on page 34 about Kant's idea of duty?
2   What are the key points raised in the dialogue on page 34 for and against duty? Add these to a copy of the table above.
3   Think about your study of the other ethical theories. Other than duty, what else might influence our moral decision-making? Add these as AO2 points to your table.

Stretch

4   Which side of the argument do you find most convincing? Arrange the points – and any others that you can think of – into an essay plan that would address the question 'Does what is right and wrong stem from the idea of duty?'
5   Write a paragraph explaining the difference between perfect and imperfect duties.

Challenge

6   Kant also suggests that there is a perfect duty to avoid suicide and an imperfect duty not to neglect the talents we have. Explain why each of these things might be the case.

3.4 Does Kant rely too much on reason?

Aim

Understand how Kantian ethics relies on human reason.

Starter

Review the terms *a priori* and *a posteriori* that you have come across in Philosophy of Religion. Write an example of an *a priori* and an *a posteriori* statement.

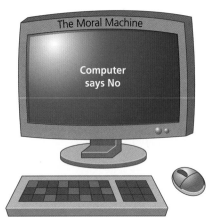

▲ Kantian ethics is often accused of being somewhat robotic in its logical method. Is this a fair criticism?

Kant and the Enlightenment

Kant is very much influenced by Enlightenment thinking and he in turn is one of its key figures. The Enlightenment was an intellectual and philosophical movement that valued reason as the source of human knowledge. There was an emphasis on scientific method and reason as the source of knowledge, as well as political ideas of liberty and tolerance. This emphasis led to a rejection of the traditional authority of Church and monarchs. It is argued that the Enlightenment sowed the seeds of the political revolutions of the nineteenth century. The motto of the Enlightenment was 'Sapere Aude' (dare to know).

Kant on reason and human nature (autonomy)

Kantian ethics relies on the accurate use of human reason. He writes at the time of the Enlightenment and is in some ways influenced by this; he also has a significant impact on the movement himself. Kant believes in the power of human beings to reason accurately and to reach answers without the need for external authorities. This influences Kant's writing on ethics and other issues in several ways. For Kant, the moral law is a product of reason. We can rationally understand the categorical imperative. He also believes that we are autonomous beings; in choosing to follow the moral law or not we are making our own free decisions.

In assessing Kant's use of reason, a number of points that have already been made about the strengths and weaknesses of Kant's ethics could be explored. Equally, there is an opportunity to draw in ideas from other topics you may have studied or will study later.

Responding to Kant

Kant's emphasis on reason is very much in keeping with his time, but it is not the only view of human nature that is available. Philosophers such as Aristotle in ancient times stressed both the rational and irrational parts of the soul. The irrational aspect, which we might associate with emotions or appetites, does seem to be a key aspect of our nature and this has featured heavily in more recent philosophy and psychology, such as in Daniel Goleman's work on emotional intelligence. This might suggest that the emotional aspects of human nature need to be equally embraced, not repressed.

Analyse and evaluate

Kant is wrong to rely on human reason because:	Kant's use of human reason can be defended because:
There are limits to human reason. Our minds experience the world through categories that we impose. We are unable to experience the 'noumena' and issues such as the existence of God are beyond our ability to provide proof.	Morality does come within the sphere of reason. Our moral duties are *a priori* synthetic; we are able to work them out using our reason.
There are valid objections to the powers of reason. Thinkers such as Barth may argue that human reason is limited and we require God's revelation in order to gain truth. If you have studied Developments in Christian Thought, Augustine's ideas of human fallenness may come into play here.	Kant believes in autonomy. Each of us has the power of reason within us. Because of this, treating persons as ends means that one of the things we owe to each other is to respect the autonomy, allowing people to reason for themselves rather than imposing our ethical ideas.
Another challenge to the reliance on reason comes from Freud. Freud argues that our moral thinking is the product of subconscious drives produced by our upbringing (see page 114–115). This would make morality more instinctive than reasoned.	Kant assumes that there is one fixed human nature and thus one way of reasoning. Hence we should each, when using our reasoning, come to the same conclusions about what the categorical imperatives are, in the same way we might reach the same conclusions when reasoning accurately about a maths question.
Situation ethics would reject the claim that ethics should be based on duty and reason. If applied in the way that Kant has in mind, reason may not give us the right answers. *Agape* love is a better motivation as far as Joseph Fletcher is concerned.	

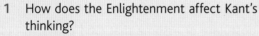

Activities

Core

1. How does the Enlightenment affect Kant's thinking?
2. What does Kant believe about our ability to reason?
3. What assumption is Kant making about human nature?

Stretch

4. The points in the left-hand column in the table above give suggested issues with Kant's reliance on reason. What might a counterargument be to each of those points? This might help you to begin to think in terms of how you would write these as paragraphs.

5. Do Kant's ethics come too much from his reliance on reason? What do you think, and why? Try to write a conclusion based on what you have read on this page and elsewhere.

Challenge

6. Kant's view on epistemology (the theory of knowledge) is known as transcendental idealism. It is complicated but worth trying to understand using an accessible source. His ideas of the noumena (thing in itself) and the phenomena (appearance) affect his whole philosophy, including his ethics.

3.5 Does Kantian ethics ultimately rely on the idea of God?

Aim

Consider the extent to which Kantian ethics is reliant on God.

Starter

You already know about duty, categorical imperative, universal law, persons as ends. Write an explanation of each of these ideas in 40–50 words each.

The case for the prosecution

Kant is **guilty** of relying on ideas of God

In order for absolute and objective moral duties to exist, Kant argues that three things must also be true. These things Kant calls postulates; they are things that must be assumed for morality to work at all.

Firstly, it is essential that human beings have free will. Kant uses the phrase 'ought implies can'. What he means by this is that when we talk in terms of moral duties – oughts and shoulds – we have to assume the person we refer to is genuinely able to do the duty in question. If we were to have no control over our own actions, we could not be held accountable for carrying out our duty.

Secondly, we must postulate (assume) the existence of an afterlife. We are required to seek the highest good (*summum bonum*). The highest good occurs when perfect virtue is rewarded by perfect happiness. It is our duty to aim for this. Because 'ought implies can', it is possible to achieve the highest good. Yet our experience of this life is that our virtuous good deeds do not always lead to good outcomes – we have all had occasions where doing the right thing seems to have made things worse. So if the highest good can be achieved, but not in this life, this means that logically we have to postulate the existence of an afterlife.

Finally, it is necessary to postulate or assume that God exists. In order that the *summum bonum* actually occurs and goodness is rewarded by happiness, there must be a God who ensures the justice of the universe.

Kant does not think that the three postulates above are proved, merely that they must be assumed practically in order for morality to exist.

Bringing God in as a required postulate seems to undermine Kant's claim that his ethical system is independent of religion and that moral duties can be rationally deduced by anyone regardless of religious belief.

The case for the defence

Kant is **not guilty** of relying on God

The prosecution case conflates two separate ethical issues. (Conflation is where you treat two separate things as if they are the same thing.) The question of 'Why do we do what we do?', which is a question about motives, is different from 'What do we gain from acting morally?', which is a question of reward.

For Kant, our motive has to be that we are doing our duty because we have worked out that it is our duty. The question of reward must not come into our motivation. The reward is merely the benefit or consequence of acting morally, it is not in itself the reason we do it.

This separates Kantian ethics from religiously motivated ethical systems such as divine command ethics, where right and wrong are based on what God says, and natural law, where the worship of God is one of the five primary precepts. In addition, a further contrast between Kantian ethics and religious moral thought is found in Kant's optimism about human nature. Unlike Augustine and others who believe humans to be fallen, Kant believes in the power of human reason to make good decisions and in human abilities to freely act on those decisions.

This shows that although Kant believes in God and thinks God may even be necessary to moral thought, the religious element does not affect the motive or the action itself.

Tip

The fact that Kant is an absolutist often leads candidates to assume that he agrees with the Ten Commandments and the teachings of Jesus. While this is true for most (but not all) commandments, stating that Kant agrees with religious teachings shows the examiner that you have not really understood the theory.

Activities

Core

1 What three things does Kant postulate (assume) for there to be objective morality?
2 What does Kant mean by the phrase 'ought implies can'?
3 Why does Kant believe that a *summum bonum* is logically necessary?

Stretch

4 How might Kant defend himself from the criticism that his ethical theory relies on the idea of God?

5 Does Kantian ethics ultimately rely on the idea of God? Write a conclusion once you have heard all the arguments.

Challenge

6 There are a number of modern philosophers who have been influenced by Kant's approach such as W.D. Ross and John Rawls. Find out more about Rawls' ideas on justice, in particular his 'veil of ignorance' or do some research on Ross' ideas of prima facie duties.

Wrap up

QUIZ

1 What is Kant's phrase for the highest good? Why does he believe in it?

2 What is Kant's phrase for a command that absolutely must be obeyed?

3 Absolutism, relativism, deontological, teleological. Which two of these words can be applied to Kant's theory?

4 What are the three tests for the categorical imperative?

5 What is a hypothetical country where everyone treats each other with dignity called?

6 What is a maxim?

7 According to Kant, should duty, inclination or consequence motivate our moral choices?

8 What is the name for a maxim that can be applied to everyone at all times?

9 What specific examples does Kant list of things that would be categorical imperatives?

10 Does Kant think that we should treat people as an end or as a means to an end?

GET READY

Summarising

1 Without looking back at the previous pages, copy and complete the table.

Key term	Explanation/definition
	Ethics should not be about inclination or consequences; actions should be motivated by this
Categorical imperative	
Hypothetical imperative	
	The first formulation of the categorical imperative
	The second formulation of the categorical imperative
Two strengths of Kantian ethics	
Two weaknesses of Kantian ethics	

Applying

2   Make a concept map on paper or use an online concept-mapping tool such as Coggle. You should ensure that you focus on both AO1 and AO2. A suggested outline is shown below, but you are free to use your own branches.

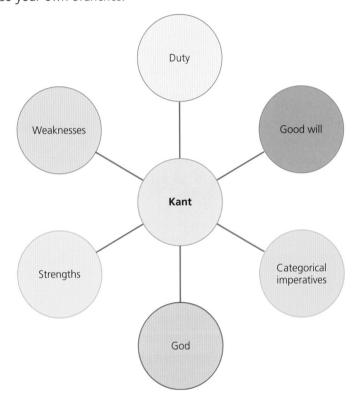

3   AO2 focus: Make a list of the strengths of Kantian ethics. Score each one out of 10 according to how persuasive you think it is. Repeat the process with the weaknesses. You could discuss your answers to this task with a friend and try to justify your views where they differ.

Going further

4   For the brave: Look at the specification on page 29 and try to write a possible exam question. Bulletpoint a model answer and get your teacher to mark it.

 Tip

Writing a good essay may begin with remembering a series of bullet points, but it is important that you can develop points fully into detailed paragraphs. This means that each point needs to be fully explained and, where appropriate, discussed and analysed.

CHECKLIST

I know, understand and can ...

☐   explain how Kant uses the idea of duty in his ethical theory

☐   explain the difference between hypothetical and categorical imperatives

☐   explain the three formulations of the categorical imperative: universal law, end in itself, and the kingdom of ends

☐   explain how Kant's ethics is based on assumptions about freedom, immortality and God

☐   assess whether Kantian ethics enables us to make good moral decisions

☐   consider whether the idea of doing your duty is what makes an action right or wrong

☐   consider criticisms of Kantian ethics such as its rejection of emotions/love and its abstract and impractical nature.

Get practising

Ask the expert

'Recently we did an essay on Kant in class. I thought I had done really well. I had explored universal law and persons as ends and considered three main evaluation points. When I spoke to Hermione, she said she had also done kingdom of ends, the three postulates, and four strengths and four weaknesses. Now I'm dreading getting the mark back. What should I do next time?' – Rachel

The expert says

When students write exam answers they often suffer from FOMiO – Fear of Missing it Out. While it is obviously a bad thing if you don't have enough material to stretch out an answer, it can sometimes be a bad thing to have too much material, particularly if we become determined to squeeze it all in somehow! This often leads to a 'buffet-type' essay – there is a little bit of everything but nothing substantial! Sometimes making the decision to leave some material out is just as important as the decision on what to leave in. In leaving things out, you are allowing space to cover the things you do include in depth.

Hermione's plan

Good will – duty - categorical and hypothetical imperatives - universal law – kingdom of ends – persons as ends – 3 postulates (God) – strengths: clear, universal law generally good, values persons, justice – weaknesses: murderer example, universalises strange imperatives, duty can be misunderstood, God required – conclusion

Task

Rewrite Hermione's plan. What would you take out? How would you organise it? Where would you add depth? Imagine you are the teacher – how would you feed back to Hermione about her essay?

Rachel's paragraph

This is one of the paragraphs from Rachel's essay, which got a higher mark than Hermione's. Read this example and practise writing similar paragraphs.

One issue with Kant's ethics is that the principle of universal law is extremely inflexible and does not work in practice. Kant is wrong to insist that we should work out what is right or wrong on the basis of whether we could logically allow all people to carry out the action. I may – because I know that a person is genuinely homeless and hungry – buy them a sandwich. However on another occasion I may not, particularly if I suspect that the person is not genuine. Kant's ethics in applying universal laws does not take into account that situations that initially seem the same can in fact be very different. This shows a fundamental weakness in this aspect of his theory.

Utilitarianism

A fourth way of making decisions about what is right and wrong is to consider the consequences in terms of how much benefit or harm results from our actions. Utilitarians argue that the right action is one that leads to the greatest good for the greatest number; one way of deciding this is to adopt the action that produces the most pleasure and/or the least amount of pain.

▲ Would you divert the tram so that only one person is killed?

Engage

Trolley problems are hypothetical thought experiments devised by the philosopher Philippa Foot (1920–2010) to show some of the contrasts between deontological and teleological ethics. In each of the problems, a person is standing next to a lever that can switch a railway car/trolley between tracks. The agent is typically required to choose between doing nothing, which leads to great harm, or taking action, which results in lesser harm, but harm for which they are directly responsible.

A utilitarian who believes in maximising pleasure and minimising pain should, in most circumstances, take action to reduce the harm caused, even if they are then directly responsible for injuries and deaths that occur.

Discuss the following trolley problems in pairs. Make a note of the factors you consider. Revisit this list after you have studied the hedonic calculus (see page 44–45).

1 The trolley is heading towards five people, but you can divert it so that it strikes an elderly drunk who is asleep on the other track.

2 The trolley is heading towards five convicted murderers but you can divert it so that it strikes a small child who is playing on the track.

3 The trolley is heading towards a Nobel Prize-winning scientist, but you can divert it so that it strikes a heavily pregnant woman.

4 The trolley is heading towards five dogs, but you can divert it so that it hits a terminally ill man.

The specification	
Content	*Key knowledge*
Utilitarianism, including: ● utility ● the hedonic calculus ● act utilitarianism ● rule utilitarianism	● The use of the significant concept of utility (seeking the greatest balance of good over evil, or pleasure over pain) in teleological and relativist approaches to ethics ● What it is (calculating the benefit or harm of an act through its consequences) and its use as a measure of individual pleasure ● What it is (calculating the consequences of each situation on its own merits) and its use in promoting the greatest amount of good over evil, or pleasure over pain ● What it is (following accepted laws that lead to the greatest overall balance of good over evil, or pleasure over pain) and its use in promoting the common good
Learners should have the opportunity to discuss issues raised by utilitarianism, including: ● whether or not utilitarianism provides a helpful method of moral decision-making ● whether or not an ethical judgement about something being good, bad, right or wrong can be based on the extent to which, in any given situation, utility is best served ● whether or not it is possible to measure good or pleasure and then reach a moral decision.	

4.1 What are the key ideas of utilitarianism?

 Aim

Understand the key ideas of utilitarianism, in particular the thoughts of Jeremy Bentham.

 Starter

You are required to hand in an essay tomorrow but have been invited to the cinema to see a film you have been looking forward to. You know that your RS teacher would be sympathetic if you lied to her and said a family emergency had stopped you from writing the essay. What would lead to the best outcome? What factors should you consider in your decision?

 Key terms

Relativism The idea that what is right or wrong is not fixed but is dependent on situation or culture

Teleological The idea that goodness is determined by the outcome of an action

Hedonistic The idea that pleasure is the true good that should be pursued

Utility principle The idea that we should do whatever is useful in terms of increasing overall good and decreasing evil

Utilitarianism – the basics

At a simple level, utilitarianism argues that the good and right thing to do is that which leads to the greatest good for the greatest number. This means that utilitarianism is a **relativist** theory: 'right' and 'wrong' are not fixed concepts at all times and in all places. Utilitarianism is also a **teleological** theory of ethics, as decisions about right and wrong are based on the outcome. For Bentham, this greater good is equated to pleasure (**hedonism**).

 Meet the thinker

▲ Jeremy Bentham (1748–1832)

Biography: Bentham was the son of a lawyer who wrote about and lived according to utilitarian principles. A social reformer, he argued against slavery, supported votes for women and suggested that homosexuality be decriminalised. Upon his death, he donated his body to scientific research and an auto-icon was made that can be seen at University College London.

Key ideas: Utilitarianism, which Bentham sees as both a political and an ethical theory.

Appears in: Utilitarianism. His ideas are also applied in Business ethics and Sexual ethics.

Utility principle

Bentham takes it as a fact of nature that human beings are motivated by pleasure and pain. We are naturally more inclined to want to do things that bring us pleasure and more likely to avoid things that cause us pain. Bentham suggests that this fact presents a simple moral rule to us: that we should do whatever leads to the greatest balance of good over evil, the thing that brings about the greatest pleasure and/or the least amount of pain. This is known as the **utility principle**. The word utility literally means usefulness, so the theory invites us to do whatever is useful to achieve this end.

Hedonic calculus

Having established the utility principle, Bentham suggests that there is almost a mathematical way of calculating the overall pleasure and pain involved. This is called the hedonic calculus. Bentham suggests that seven factors need to be considered when making a moral decision. For the possible pains and pleasures, we need to consider:

Tip

Utilitarianism is not a selfish ethical theory as some people think. When properly applied, it is actually very demanding. I cannot just consider my own preferences, pleasures or pains. I have to consider everyone.

- **Intensity:** How strong is the pleasure or pain that is involved?
- **Duration:** How long will the pleasure or pain last?
- **Certainty:** How sure are we that the anticipated pleasure or pain will occur?
- **Propinquity** (closeness or proximity): How soon will the pleasure or pain occur?
- **Fecundity:** How likely is that the pleasure will lead to further pleasures?
- **Purity:** How likely is it that pain will result from the original pleasure?
- **Extent:** How many people will be affected?

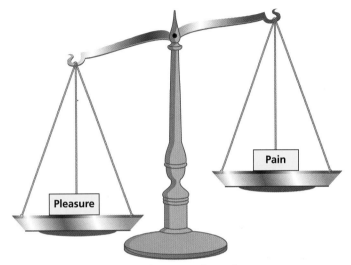

▲ Utilitarianism measures pleasure against pain

This method of considering pain and pleasure requires that we consider long-term consequences: fecundity and duration ensure that we should not seek short-term pleasure at the expense of long-term pain. It is also worth noting that utilitarianism is not a selfish ethical theory – the focus on purity and extent requires that we consider how each individual might be affected by our actions.

Activities

Core

1. What is Bentham's principle of utility?
2. What 'two masters' does Bentham believe that we have been given by nature?
3. Explain three of the aspects of the hedonic calculus.

Stretch

4. Rewrite Bentham's key quote on utility in your own words.
5. Look again at the Starter activity. Apply each of the factors of the hedonic calculus. What decision would lead to the best outcome?

Challenge

6. Bentham's ideas are found in *An Introduction to the Principles of Morals and Legislation*. The text is readily available online. Try reading Chapters 1 and 4 carefully. Add a few useful quotes to your notes.

4.2 Is utilitarianism a helpful way of making moral decisions?

Aim

Develop an understanding of the key ideas of Mill's utilitarianism and consider whether utilitarianism is a good approach to making moral decisions.

Starter

You are exploring an underground cave with a group of friends. The waters rise and you make your way to the only remaining exit. Your friend Big Jake goes first, but gets stuck. You are all likely to drown unless Jake can be dislodged from the hole. You have a stick of dynamite with which you could blow Jake out of the hole, but which would kill him. Alternatively, you could all drown and the water would force Jake through the hole to safety. Use Bentham's utilitarianism to solve this dilemma – what else might you need to know?

▲ Bentham believed that push penny and poetry were equally valuable

The swine ethic objection

One common objection to utilitarianism is that it is a 'swine ethic' – an ethic that treats us as if we were pigs. It assumes that we are creatures that value each pleasure identically. Bentham himself claimed that the game of push penny – a simple children's game – was just as pleasurable as poetry, yet this does not seem right. Equally, it has also been noted that in Bentham's utilitarianism, actions as horrific as gang rape could be supported as the pleasure of the multiple rapists would outweigh the pain of the victim. While Bentham would not have intended to imply this, it seems difficult to see how his system can avoid this criticism.

? Meet the thinker

▲ John Stuart Mill (1806–73)

Biography: John Stuart Mill was a child genius whose father was a close friend of Jeremy Bentham. He was interested in social justice and politics as well as ethics. His classic works include *On Liberty* (1859). His marriage to Harriet Taylor, his intellectual equal, reinforced his desire to argue for women's rights. He also served as a Liberal MP towards the end of his life.

Key ideas: Utilitarianism, the non-harm principle and equal rights for women.

Appears in: This topic as well as Business ethics and Sexual ethics.

Mill to the rescue

John Stuart Mill's utilitarianism aims to correct what he sees as a major defect in the idea left by Bentham. Bentham's utilitarianism is quantitative and appears to suggest that we can coldly calculate the pleasures and pains involved in each situation. Mill is more interested in the quality of each pleasure. He argues that there are two types of pleasures:

- **Higher pleasures:** These are intellectual and social pleasures that only human beings can enjoy, such as intellectual conversation or enjoyment of art.
- **Lower pleasures:** These are pleasures of the body that both humans and other creatures enjoy, such as food, sleep and sex.

While a creature such as a pig enjoys quite simple pleasures – for example eating leftover food and rolling in mud – we are capable of higher pleasures. It is possible for us to appreciate music and art as well as engage in political and philosophical discourse. Mill argues that all competent judges who have experienced both types of pleasure will argue that the higher pleasures are more important. Hence for Mill the gang rape example fails because the rapists experience a lower pleasure that can never outweigh the trauma and pain caused.

'It is better to be a human being dissatisfied than a pig satisfied; better to be Socrates dissatisfied than a fool satisfied. And if the fool, or the pig, are of a different opinion, it is because they know only their own side of the question.'
(John Stuart Mill, *Utilitarianism*)

Mill recognises that the quantitative utilitarianism of Bentham risks allowing the 'tyranny of the majority', where the pleasure of the majority can justify ignoring the suffering of a minority. In *On Liberty*, he writes about the non-harm principle. Mill believes that each individual should be free to live as they choose, so long as they do not cause harm to others. Indeed, he argues that the only reason a government should introduce a law is to prevent harm to others.

Analyse and evaluate

Utilitarianism is a helpful way of making moral decisions because:	Utilitarianism is not a helpful way of making moral decisions because:
Utilitarianism (particularly Bentham's version) is relatively straightforward in the sense that the key idea is not difficult to understand or apply, *but* ... (See weakness 1)	(From strength 1) ... although the idea of utilitarianism is straightforward, the application of the theory is anything but straightforward. There are so many factors and variables to consider. It is also difficult to know how far to take the consequences of an action. Sometimes a simple decision may have repercussions that affect future generations.
It is difficult to object to the basic principle that happiness is a good thing. We would not find many people, if any, who would sincerely argue that they do not want to be happy. This suggests that utilitarianism at least has a good aim.	Similar to the above, utilitarianism requires that we are able to make a reasonable prediction as to the outcome of an action. However, it is not always obvious what the effects of telling the truth vs telling a lie are in any given circumstance. We cannot predict the future.
Utilitarianism is a secular ethical theory and does not rely on God or other metaphysical ideas that cannot be proved in order to justify its decisions.	While everyone is considered, the greatest good for the greatest number inevitably leads to poorer treatment of minority groups and may disregard rights to serve the greater good. Bentham himself famously refers to rights as 'nonsense on stilts'.
Utilitarianism is democratic in that everyone counts equally regardless of whom they are; each person's potential pains or pleasures are to be considered. Additionally, the theory requires that we are impartial in our decision-making and do not count those nearer to us, such as our family, as more significant than a stranger.	It is difficult to measure pain and pleasure (see page 45).
	Utilitarianism also disregards moral agency. In his thought experiment 'Jim and the Indians', Bernard Williams gives a situation where a utilitarian can save ten lives by killing one person themselves. He argues that even if this were the right thing to do, we would find it difficult. This is because we are moral agents who have to live with ourselves after the act.

Activities

Core

1 What is meant by the claim that utilitarianism is a swine ethic?

2 How does Mill's view of pleasure differ from that of Bentham?

3 What is the 'non-harm principle'?

Stretch

4 Examine the weaknesses of utilitarianism shown in the table. How many of these weaknesses affect only Bentham? Which affect both thinkers?

5 Look at the quote from John Stuart Mill. Explain it in your own words.

Challenge

6 Use the internet to find out more about Williams' example of Jim and the Indians. What happens in the story? What point is Williams making? Do you think he is right? Why or why not?

4.3 Is act or rule utilitarianism better?

Aim

Learn about the differences between act and rule utilitarianism and consider which view makes the most sense.

Starter

Sort the following terms and phrases into two columns depending on whether they refer to Bentham or Mill. Can you explain each of the terms?

Hedonic calculus, qualitative view of pleasure, non-harm principle, quantitative view of pleasure, higher and lower pleasures, swine ethic.

Tip

One common oversimplification of utilitarianism is that it is almost like having a hands-up vote. For example, if five people want X but only two people want Y, then X is good. This is not what utilitarianism is saying. The other factors in Bentham's hedonic calculus or Mill's higher and lower pleasures may mean that the effect on the minority is so great that there are very good reasons for choosing Y.

Key terms

Act utilitarianism The idea that we should always perform the act that leads to the greatest balance of good over evil
Rule utilitarianism The idea that we should always follow the rule that generally leads to the greatest balance of good over evil for society rather than the individual

Two different approaches to achieving the greatest good for the greatest number or the greatest balance of good over evil are taken by act and rule utilitarianism.

I judge each situation separately to determine what leads to most happiness.

I believe there are general principles that typically lead to the greater good.

▲ One of the thinkers above is an act utilitarian and the other is a rule utilitarian. Can you identify which is which?

Act utilitarianism

Act utilitarianism aims to produce the best balance of good over evil in each case. It takes situations on a case-by-case basis. Bentham's hedonic calculus is a good example of such an approach. This means that the act utilitarian may well give different answers to the same action, depending on the situation or context. For example, there may be greater happiness produced by telling your friend the correct directions to the shop if they need to purchase some essential goods. Yet telling the truth would not be appropriate if the school bully asks where the person he wishes to beat up is hiding.

Rule utilitarianism

Rule utilitarianism also aims at the greatest balance of good over evil, but it has the common good of society rather than individuals as its starting point. It suggests that we do on the whole know the actions that typically lead to happiness and pleasure – we know that stealing tends to cause more misery to the victims than pleasure to the thief (particularly if the thief ends up in prison), so we are able to make a utilitarian rule that 'stealing is wrong'. It is worth noting that unlike other rule-based ethical theories, the rules are not fixed. The basis of the rules is entirely utilitarian – the greater good or greatest happiness – hence the rules can be changed if society changes.

Strong and weak rule utilitarianism

A further distinction within rule utilitarianism is the difference between strong and weak versions of the theory. A strong rule utilitarian would argue that once we have decided the rules that lead to the greatest good, these rules are fixed and cannot, under any circumstances, be broken.

A weak rule utilitarian would make allowances for exceptions. While the rules do broadly lead to the greatest good and should generally be followed, there may be exceptional cases that require a rule to be broken.

There is some debate as to whether Mill would align himself with act or rule utilitarianism (the categories are later terms that were not applied during his time). He argues that the past experience of human beings does allow us to know the tendencies of actions. His principles of liberty and non-harm are rules or principles that would seem to allow society to flourish, so he is perhaps best seen as a rule utilitarian. He is, however, aware of the problem posed by Kant of the murderer seeking his next victim (see page 33) and it is Mill's view that it would be sensible to lie in that situation, hence weak rule utilitarianism seems to be his broad position.

Analyse and evaluate

Act utilitarianism is a better approach to moral decision-making because:	*Rule utilitarianism is a better approach to moral decision-making because:*
The case-by-case decision-making of act utilitarianism is a strength as it allows flexibility, recognising that no two situations are the same. However, the other side of this coin is that compared to rule utilitarianism it takes considerable time to weigh up all the complex factors in each situation.	Rule utilitarianism offers a quicker approach to decision-making, recognising that case-by-case decision-making is unnecessary and very time-consuming. However, there can be situations where different utilitarian rules and principles clash and a different approach would be needed to decide between the rules.
It could be argued that rule utilitarianism is an incoherent position, particularly in weak rule utilitarianism, as the theory ends up collapsing into act utilitarianism anyway as more and more exceptions are allowed (J.J.C. Smart).	Rule utilitarianism allows us to make rules that uphold justice and rights, two things that may be lost in individual cases for the act utilitarian. The McCloskey example, where a sheriff chooses to arrest an innocent man for the greater good, would be allowed by an act utilitarian but cannot be justified by a rule utilitarian as persistent unjust acts would undermine justice itself.

Activities

Core

1 What is the main difference between act and rule utilitarianism?
2 What is the difference between strong and weak rule utilitarianism?
3 Look at the table above assessing utilitarianism. Which of the points criticising Bentham might not apply to rule utilitarianism? Add these to your notes.

Stretch

4 Explain why Smart believes that rule utilitarianism collapses into act utilitarianism. Is this a bad thing?
5 Write a conclusion to an essay question that asks whether act or rule utilitarianism is better.

Challenge

6 Find out more about the McCloskey problem. How does this example show that utilitarianism has a problem with justice?

4.4 Can pleasure, happiness or goodness be measured?

Aim

Consider the objection that utilitarianism is flawed as we are unable to measure pleasure or happiness.

Starter

Without looking at your notes, write for 15 minutes explaining all that you know about utilitarianism so far. This can be prose or bullet points. You should aim to have a balance between AO1 and AO2.

Should I kick Vicious Vince the school bully?

Pros:
My enjoyment (2 hedons)
His victims' brief pleasure (10 x 1 hedon)

Cons:
My considerable pain later (5 hedons)
My parents' sadness at my suspension from school (2 x 3 hedons)

▲ Utilitarianism seems to imply that calculations such as this are possible

Vic: Will you stop playing that wretched game and do something to help me get ready for the party!

Rick: But aligning the sweets on screen brings me considerable pleasure, and in any case you have been stuck in your pointless book all morning.

Vic: It is certainly not pointless; this is great literature and is easily worth twice your Candy Crush.

Rick: I just don't see how you can get into Henry V when you haven't read the first four. I for one have never enjoyed anything by Bill Shakestick.

Vic: It's Shakespeare. By the way, have you sorted the playlist for the party yet? Julian Waterfield is coming and he only listens to classical music. He says chart music causes him actual pain and distress.

Rick: I'm not sure that matters – both Karen and Chris quite enjoy modern music.

Vic: 'Quite enjoy' doesn't make up for extreme pain but it's too late now. Did you download the latest 'Hey that sounds a lot like music' album?

Rick: No, I gave the £10 to a charity as it seemed that I would help more people to avoid pain and distress than the few people who might actually come to our party.

Vic: I suppose Julian will also be pleased then.

Measuring pleasure

One argument in favour of the notion that we can to some extent measure pleasure or goodness comes from John Stuart Mill. He argues that if we want to know what is good and desirable, we should look at what people actually desire. The fact is that people do seek pleasure and happiness; they pursue it as an end in itself and everything else in life that is desirable is desirable only because it contributes to the goal of happiness. So, this simple observation of reality does tell us that happiness is in fact a good thing and that it should be pursued.

Mill offers an analogy to reinforce his point. If we want to know what is or isn't visible, the only way we can prove this is by asking what can actually be seen. In the same way, we can only resolve what is desirable by asking what people actually desire. Other thinkers have expressed some reservations about this 'proof'. What people desire or aim towards can indeed be described, but this does not establish the normative claim that this ought to be desired. Perhaps we can measure people's happiness in the sense of what they desire, but this does not necessarily mean those desires are good.

The distribution problem

One subtle variation related to the difficulty of measuring pleasure and pain (mentioned earlier in section 4.1) is the distribution problem. Assuming that we can in some way measure pleasure, this raises the problem that we may create the same overall amount of happiness or pleasure, but that this pleasure may be distributed quite differently.

If we imagine that decision A would lead to person X being much happier (let's say by 10 hedons) and persons Y and Z each being slightly happier (by 1 hedon each), then the decision generates 12 hedons of happiness. However, we could reach the same overall happiness by decision B, which would give 4 hedons to each person. In theory the amount of happiness is the same overall, yet the two outcomes feel very different.

Philosophers argue that this actually reinforces the criticism that it is difficult, if not impossible, to measure pleasure and pain in the way that utilitarians hope.

Analyse and evaluate

It can be argued that pleasure, happiness or goodness can be measured because:	*It can be argued that pleasure, happiness or goodness cannot be measured because:*
Mill's argument that happiness is desirable rests on the assumption that we can observe what people desire and thus presumably have some measure of whether they are achieving these desires. Hence, on a crude level we may be able to have some measure of pleasure or pain.	Things that are measurable or quantifiable tend to have units of measurement. Time has hours and minutes, mass has grams, etc. There are no obvious units that could measure pleasure or pain.
Preference versions of utilitarianism may avoid some of the difficulties of measuring pleasure as they would argue that overall utility/happiness lies in preference satisfaction. We may be able through surveys and other empirical research to ascertain the relative happiness of people in terms of achieving their life goals.	Further difficulties in the measurement of pleasure and pain lie in the fact that pleasure and pain are often subjective to the individual. We enjoy different things and each of us may have a different pain threshold and be willing to suffer more pain for a greater good. This would suggest that if any version of utilitarianism is to succeed, it would have to be one such as preference utilitarianism that does not require such a measurement.
As neuroscience advances it may be possible to measure happiness or pleasure in terms of observing what is happening in the brain during key moments. While we are perhaps some way off having portable brain scanners permanently attached to us, the existence of such technology would make measurement of pleasure possible.	Assuming pleasure and pain can be measured would require a very simple version of utilitarianism such as Bentham's, where 'push penny is as good as poetry'. Yet Mill seems right that there are higher and lower pleasures. How should the higher pleasures be weighted? Are they worth twice the lower pleasures, or three or four times?
	Nozick's experience machine and Moore's (see page 98) open question argument both raise the possibility that even if we actually could measure pleasure, we are not necessarily measuring the good.

Activities

Core

1. What three criticisms of utilitarianism are suggested in the dialogue?
2. How could neuroscience help us to measure pleasure and pain?
3. What is the difficulty in trying to measure higher and lower pleasures?

Stretch

4. How does Mill attempt to offer a proof of utilitarianism? How successful is this proof? Justify your answer.

5. How does preference utilitarianism (see page 52) potentially avoid the issue of the need to measure pleasure?

Challenge

6. Write a continuation of the dialogue in which different forms of utilitarianism are discussed.

4.5 Should ethical judgements be based on a concept such as utility?

Starter

Without speaking to anyone else, write down in order the five things in life that you consider to be most valuable, for example health, love, riches. Compare your list with a partner's. Does pleasure feature on any of your lists? Where does it come?

Key quote

'the utilitarian position is a minimal one ... that we reach by universalising self-interested decision-making.' (Peter Singer, *Practical Ethics*)

Utility is not necessarily pleasure

Utilitarianism comes in many forms, some of which are dependent on pleasure and some are not. The theory broadly states that an action is good and right if more good (utility) is produced by this action than the other alternatives. As we have seen, however, measuring pleasure and pain is difficult if not impossible. Hence in addition to the hedonistic versions of utilitarianism seen in the work of Bentham and Mill, other views of utility are possible. Some modern utilitarians think the focus on pleasure is too narrow. The idea that pleasure isn't the most valuable thing to pursue seems to be demonstrated by Nozick's thought experiment of the experience machine (see below).

It may also be worth observing that even if utility is understood as pleasure, this need not be a bad thing. Mill's focus on higher and lower pleasures leads to the development of the non-harm principle which suggests that in order to secure the pleasure of most individuals, society should only adopt laws that prevent harm to others. This principle has been adopted by various political thinkers over the last 100 years.

Singer's preference utilitarianism

One popular form of modern utilitarianism is preference utilitarianism, as held by philosopher Peter Singer (1946–) and others. Preference utilitarianism recognises that different people have different views about what happiness is. We have different aims in life and different things that we consider important. These are our preferences or interests. Preference utilitarianism argues that people should be allowed to pursue their preferences as long as this does not interfere with anyone else's pursuit of happiness. Hence the morally good thing to do is that which maximises the satisfaction of the preferences and interests of the most people. In doing this we have to imagine ourselves as 'impartial observers', free from our personal biases and considering what each individual would truly want

Singer argues that the preferences of all persons should be taken into account. His most famous work has been around animal rights issues and he argues that many species of animal satisfy the criteria to be described as persons. Although they cannot articulate their preferences, we can consider their interests and assume what they would desire – just as a parent might do for a small infant or a relative might do for a severely disabled person. The fact that they cannot communicate preferences does not stop us as impartial observers from acting in their interests.

One advantage of this form of utilitarianism is that it may be easier to measure. In addition, it allows individuals to pursue their own interests and not be restricted to whatever the majority deems to be happiness. Hence it avoids the 'tyranny of the majority' (a problem for Bentham). We also retain the flexibility of resolving different cases and issues differently as we are not tied to rule utilitarianism.

Tip

Although Singer's preference utilitarianism is not specifically mentioned on the specification, it can be used as a useful way of providing a contrast and thus assessing other forms of utilitarianism.

Singer's later work

More recently, Singer has moved closer to a more hedonistic view of utilitarianism, one that is more focused on avoiding pain. In *The Life You Can Save*, he argues that it is morally wrong for us not to donate to charities that work to alleviate extreme poverty in the world; we may not be able to save everyone ourselves, but by doing without a few luxury items we may be able to save a child's life.

Nozick's experience machine

One powerful objection to hedonistic versions of utilitarianism has come from Robert Nozick's thought experiment on the experience machine. Nozick asks us to consider the possibility that scientists invent a machine that you can step into that will give you every possible pleasurable sensation you could ever wish to experience – the taste of pizza, birds singing, the feeling of getting an A on an exam – without actually having any real-life experiences. Nozick suggests that most of us would decline the offer of being plugged into such a machine as we value our real-life experiences far more. This seems to show that pleasure is not the ultimate thing that we aim for in life.

Analyse and evaluate

Utility is a good basis for making moral judgements because:	Utility is a poor basis for making moral judgements because:
Utilitarianism has been progressive and the arguments based on these principles have been used to decriminalise homosexuality, ban slavery and give votes to women.	Nozick's experience machine seems to show that if utility is understood in terms of pleasure, this is not the thing that is most important to us.
The idea of utility gives a decision procedure. Some other ethical theories such as Kantian ethics may promise clarity, but when duties clash there is no easy way of resolving the issue. Utility provides a way of resolving each dilemma.	If we assume that utility is something similar to preference satisfaction then it is unclear whose preferences do or do not count, for example infants, dogs, snails.
Similarly, utilitarianism offers a pragmatism that works in the real world, whereas other ethical theories offer theoretical solutions that do not work in practice.	Preference satisfaction is not easily quantifiable and as such this version goes against the spirit of utilitarianism.
See also the key strengths and weaknesses of utilitarianism discussed elsewhere in this chapter – some of which are also relevant here.	Utility is too demanding. Greater happiness is always achieved by giving money and resources to the poorest rather than buying oneself a coffee or taking out a subscription for the latest films. It becomes morally wrong to give ourselves such treats.
	It may also be possible to argue that other motivations, such as duty, *agape* or *telos*, represent better moral motivations.

Activities

Core

1. How does preference utilitarianism differ from hedonistic versions?
2. Why does Singer think that animals need to be included in utilitarian calculations?
3. How have Singer's views changed in recent years?

Stretch

4. Write an AO2 paragraph using Nozick's thought experiment on the pleasure machine. Is his point correct? Why or why not?

5. Is utility a better approach to ethics than appealing to the concept of duty? Write a paragraph justifying your answer.

Challenge

6. Find out more about the work of Peter Singer by looking at his website or watching his TED talk on the life that you can save.

4.6 The Big Debate: Do we need rules in ethics? (Absolutism vs relativism)

Aim

Draw together everything you have learned in the four chapters on Ethical Theories and use it to discuss the importance of rules in ethics.

Starter

Without looking at your notes, explain or define the following terms: absolutism; relativism; deontological; teleological; utilitarianism; natural law; Kantian ethics; situation ethics.

At the end of the task, check your understanding by comparing what you have written against your notes or this textbook.

Preparing the case

Given that each situation we face may be very different, are rules really the best way to resolve ethical dilemmas?

The case for the prosecution

Rules are not needed in ethics: Case for relativism

Evidence for rejection of rules might include the following thinkers or ideas:

Joseph Fletcher: One of the key principles of my situation ethics is that of relativism. While love may be to some extent an absolute, the way it is applied varies by situation and this means rules aren't always helpful.

Jeremy Bentham: My hedonic calculus suggests that we need to carefully weigh up the pleasure and pain caused in different situations and come to a conclusion.

John Stuart Mill: My utilitarianism has some place for general rules, but decision-making is largely based on my view of higher and lower pleasures. Higher pleasures are those intellectual and social pleasures that all competent judges would prefer.

Peter Singer: One of the problems with absolutist ethics is that it treats us all the same. We are different and we may have different preferences and aims in life.

The case for the defence

Rules are needed in ethics: Case for absolutism

Evidence for needing rules might include the following thinkers/ideas:

> **Immanuel Kant:** The principle of universal law is important, because without it each of us may be tempted to see ourselves as an exception. This means we effectively treat others as objects.

> **Thomas Aquinas:** We are able to rationally work out primary precepts and secondary precepts that should apply to all people and help us to flourish as human beings.

> **The innocent victim** in the McCloskey paradox (page 49): Focus on utility is dangerous, as some people will inevitably suffer when we ignore the moral rules.

I'll see you in court

You can work through the process below individually either verbally or in written form (sometimes verbalising thoughts is the first step to being able to write them down), or you could work through the activities as a group or class, debating and reaching a verdict.

The judge opens the case: What are the key distinctions in Ethics? What are absolutism and relativism? How do deontological and teleological approaches differ? What are the key issues?

The case for the prosecution is presented: Rules are NOT helpful in Ethics. What are the key arguments in favour of this view? What key evidence would be presented?

Defence cross-examination: What are the issues arising from this evidence? What counterarguments can be brought forward?

The case for the defence is presented: Rules ARE helpful in Ethics. What are the key arguments in favour of this view? What key evidence would be presented?

Prosecution cross-examination: What are the issues arising from this evidence? What counterarguments can be brought forward?

Closing speeches: What is the key piece of evidence for the prosecution case? What is the key piece of evidence for the defence case?

Jury decision: What conclusion do you reach? Why? (If you are doing this exercise as a class/group, you can take a vote.)

Activities

Core

1 Create a large concept map that outlines the case in favour of relativism.

2 Create a large concept map that outlines the case in favour of absolutism.

3 Write a speech to use in the court case – select one of the arguments or scholars. Make your speech persuasive by adding justified reasons and examples to support your view.

Stretch

4 Write questions to ask the defence and prosecution witnesses. Make them as tricky as possible.

5 Think about possible answers to your questions – how could you respond and challenge the witness further? (This is developing the skill of critical analysis found in AO2 Level 6.)

Challenge

6 If you have enjoyed this debate, you could carry out a further debate looking at whether religious or secular approaches to ethics are better. This would involve putting natural law and situation ethics on one side against Kantian ethics and utilitarianism on the other.

Wrap up

QUIZ

1 What is the name of Bentham's method of calculating right and wrong?

2 What does it mean to describe utilitarianism as a teleological approach to ethics?

3 What is the name given to the idea that we should make decisions based on what leads to the greatest good in each individual situation?

4 What is the literal meaning of the word 'utility'?

5 Which thinker believes that there are higher and lower pleasures?

6 Whose version of utilitarianism has been criticised as being a swine ethic?

7 What is the difference between strong and weak rule utilitarianism?

8 What criticism of utilitarianism is being made in Williams' story of 'Jim and the Indians'?

9 What are the two 'sovereign masters' that nature has put over us, according to Bentham?

10 What is preference utilitarianism?

GET READY

Summarising

1 Make a copy of the grid below. Without looking at your notes, aim to fill in the boxes by making four or five points in each box. You could further train your memory by trying to repeat the process after a couple of weeks.

Hedonic calculus	Utility principle	Act utilitarianism
Rule utilitarianism	Differences between Bentham and Mill	Key strengths of utilitarianism
Key weaknesses of utilitarianism	My conclusion about utilitarianism	An area I need to find out about/do more work on …

2 Below are six words that can be used to describe ethical theories. What does each of the words mean? Which would you use to describe the theory of utilitarianism? Explain your answer.

Religious, Secular, Absolutist, Relativist, Deontological, Teleological

3 AO2 focus: Make a list of the strengths of utilitarianism. Score each one out of ten according to how persuasive you think it is. Repeat the process with the weaknesses. You could discuss your answers to this task with a friend, trying to justify your views where they differ.

Debate

4 'Making decisions based on the greatest happiness for everyone is the best way to do ethics.'

Discuss this in small groups and make a note of the points raised. Add them to your notes.

Going further

5 For the brave: Look at the specification on page 43 and try to write a possible exam question. Bulletpoint a model answer and get your teacher to mark it.

CHECKLIST

I know, understand and can ...

- [ ] explain the ideas of utility and the hedonic calculus
- [ ] explain the theories of act utilitarianism and rule utilitarianism
- [ ] assess whether utilitarianism enables us to make good moral decisions
- [ ] consider the extent to which utility is the thing to consider in moral decision-making
- [ ] consider issues with utilitarianism, including whether it is possible to measure pleasure and pain.

Get practising

Ask the expert

'I struggle a lot with conclusions when I'm writing essays. I try to stick to the time limit but find myself rushing the conclusion. My teacher has also said that my conclusions tend not to be focused, but I'm not too sure what she means.' – Liv

Liv's conclusion

In conclusion, utilitarianism has lots of different strengths and weaknesses. Bentham's version uses the hedonic calculus whereas Mill's version uses higher and lower pleasures. Each of these helps utilitarians make moral decisions so there are good arguments on both sides.

Liv's conclusion suffers from a number of issues. Firstly, it is quite rushed; it is important that you ensure that you have 5 minutes at the end of the essay to write a good conclusion. Second, this conclusion is AO1-focused and largely sums up what utilitarianism is rather than advancing an argument. Finally, it is inconclusive in that no decision has been reached about utilitarianism. Sarah's conclusion below shows some of the elements you would find in a good conclusion.

Writing a good conclusion

A good conclusion should draw together the argument that you have been making as the essay has progressed. It shouldn't be a surprise, as each of your paragraphs will hopefully have given some indication which way you are arguing.

Your conclusion will highlight some of the key judgements you have already made as you have gone through the essay and will address the specific wording of the question. In your conclusion, do not introduce a whole new topic or suddenly bring in new material you have not previously discussed or unpacked in the essay, as this may seem like you have lost focus.

Sarah's conclusion

While it may appear that the democratic nature of utilitarianism would mean that there is equality and that each person's happiness is valued, the reality is quite different. The treatment of minorities in Bentham's utilitarianism means that the theory doesn't produce the equality it seems to promise. While Mill and Singer may have some response to this, they are unable to address further weaknesses such as the need to be able to work out future consequences of our actions, so overall utilitarianism does not help us make good moral decisions.

The expert says

Like the rest of your essay, the conclusion needs to show that you have given an answer. Look at the specific wording of the question and make sure that the conclusion in particular shows that you have addressed the question asked. If the question asks something specific – for example, whether it is possible for utilitarians to measure pleasure and pain – then the conclusion does need to focus on this issue (as does the essay in general!). A conclusion that seems to give a general assessment of utilitarianism may indicate that the whole answer lacks focus.

CHAPTER 5

Euthanasia

Big picture

Some of the most interesting and challenging issues currently being debated in ethics are found in the area of medical ethics. The discussion and debate over euthanasia is one of these topics.

Engage

In April 1989, Tony Bland was critically injured in the Hillsborough Stadium disaster. He was left in a deep coma known as a persistent vegetative state (PVS), had very limited brain activity and had no prospect of recovering. Doctors would not turn off his life-support machine as it was certainly against the law and would break the Hippocratic Oath that doctors take to preserve life, meaning they would face prosecution for ending his life. Tony's parents went through various legal stages before the High Court ruled that Tony's treatment could be withdrawn. He died on 3 March 1992.

Euthanasia is essentially illegal in the UK and the case above is unusual. Find out more about the case. What was it that made the case unusual?

Following your research, discuss the case in pairs. What is your reaction and what questions are raised? Are there things in the paragraph above that you wish to clarify? Write these questions down. You can return to them once you are further on in the topic.

Key term

Euthanasia Literally meaning a good death, it refers to the practice of hastening someone's death perhaps in order to spare them further suffering

The specification

Content	Key knowledge
Key ideas of euthanasia, including: ● sanctity of life ● quality of life ● voluntary euthanasia ● non-voluntary euthanasia	● The religious origins of this concept (that human life is made in God's image and is therefore sacred in value) ● The secular origins of this significant concept (that human life has to possess certain attributes in order to have value) ● What it is (that a person's life is ended at their request or with their consent) and its use in the case of incurable or terminal illness ● What it is (that a person's life is ended without their consent but with the consent of someone representing their interests) and its use in the case of a patient who is in a persistent vegetative state

Learners should have the opportunity to discuss issues raised by euthanasia, including:
● the application of natural law and situation ethics to euthanasia
● whether or not the religious concept of sanctity of life has any meaning in twenty-first-century medical ethics
● whether or not a person should or can have complete autonomy over their own life and decisions made about it
● whether or not there is a moral difference between medical intervention to end a patient's life and medical non-intervention to end a patient's life.

5.1 Does the idea of sanctity of life still apply in the twenty-first century?

Aim

Learn about the sanctity of life and consider whether this concept is still appropriate for the twenty-first century.

Starter

Look at the definitions given below of voluntary euthanasia and non-voluntary euthanasia. What moral issues are raised by each type of euthanasia? Is there a significant difference that might make one form of euthanasia harder to justify?

Key terms

Voluntary euthanasia When a person's life is ended at their request or with their consent
Non-voluntary euthanasia When a person's life is ended without their consent but with the consent of someone representing their interests, e.g. when the person is in a persistent vegetative state
Sanctity of life A religious concept that human life is made in God's image and is therefore sacred in value
Quality of life A largely secular idea that human life has to possess certain attributes in order to have value

Understanding sanctity of life

Both **voluntary euthanasia** and **non-voluntary euthanasia** seem to contradict the religious belief in the **sanctity of life**. This is a belief in the value and sacredness of life that is shared by many religious believers. In Christianity, this value comes from being created in the image of God. This means that it is morally wrong to take life. There are a number of biblical texts that support belief in the sanctity of life:

● 'So God created mankind in his own image, in the image of God he created them.' (Genesis 1:27): The 'image of God' may refer to the capacity for rationality or the ability to make moral decisions. It is this divine image that gives human life its value.

● 'You shall not murder.' (Exodus 20:13): The command against taking a life is one of the Ten Commandments. Whether euthanasia is murder or whether the text should be translated in terms of killing more generally may be a matter of debate.

● 'The Lord gave, and the Lord has taken away; blessed be the name of the Lord.' (Job 1:21): It is for God to decide the moment of birth and the moment of death; it cannot be a human decision as our lives are not our own but God's.

● 'Do you not know that your bodies are temples of the Holy Spirit, who is in you, whom you have received from God.' (1 Corinthians 6:18): Paul in the New Testament also reinforces the idea that the believer's body in a sense belongs to God as the giver of life.

Catholic Christians place weight on the natural law and the teachings of the Church in addition to biblical evidence. In natural law, the primary precept of preserving innocent life establishes the importance of the sanctity of life. In addition, the Church has officially pronounced against euthanasia, particularly in the 1980 Declaration on Euthanasia.

Quality of life

Whereas some thinkers prioritise sanctity of life in medical ethics, others view **quality of life** as more significant. The quality of life principle takes the view that whether life is valuable depends on whether it is worth living; it needs to have certain characteristics in order to be valuable, for example happiness, autonomy or freedom from pain. The utilitarian philosopher

Peter Singer argues for replacing the traditional sanctity of life ethics with five quality of life commandments:

1 We should recognise that the worth of human life varies.
2 We should take responsibility for the consequences of our decisions to save or end life.
3 We should respect a person's desire to live or die.
4 We should only bring children into the world if they are wanted.
5 We should not discriminate on the basis of species.

The ethical theory of situation ethics typically favours quality of life over sanctity of life in dealing with issues such as euthanasia.

Analyse and evaluate

The concept of sanctity of life remains a useful concept because:	*The concept of sanctity of life is no longer useful because:*
It upholds the intrinsic value of life in a culture where we increasingly dehumanise others through our interactions in the real world and online.	Sanctity of life is a religious concept that is out of place in an increasingly secular society. It is estimated that over 50 per cent of people in the UK no longer believe in God and less than 10 per cent regularly attend church.
The sanctity of life ensures that basic rights such as the right to life are respected, particularly in cases where those involved are not able to speak up for themselves.	The concept of sanctity of life seems to be at odds with people's autonomy in cases of voluntary euthanasia, where people who have sufficient mental capacity may request death.
Those who campaign against euthanasia worry about the potential of a slippery slope – that even some forms of euthanasia are permitted may lead to pressure being put upon the vulnerable, such as the elderly or disabled. They point to a similar decline in respect for life when abortion was legalised. It was anticipated that a few thousand cases would occur each year on medical grounds, yet currently over 180,000 terminations take place each year in the UK. In terms of euthanasia, campaigners worry about a growth in cases.	Interpreting sanctity of life as saving life at all costs is self-defeating. It leads to people dying in horrible pain and does not ultimately treat human life with dignity and respect.
	Sanctity of life demands that all life must be saved at all costs. But given medical and technological advances, we are now far better placed to know where treatment may lead to improvement and where it is pointless. We do not have to treat all people.

Activities

Core

1 Explain what is meant by voluntary and non-voluntary euthanasia. Give an example of each.
2 Explain how the Bible may be said to support the idea of sanctity of life.
3 Why might a natural law thinker support the idea of sanctity of life?

Stretch

4 Look at Singer's quality of life commands. Which ones are relevant to the topic of euthanasia? How would they be applied?

5 Look at the table above. Which of the arguments for or against the usefulness of the concept of sanctity of life do you find the most convincing? Give a reason for your answer.

Challenge

6 'Intentionally causing one's own death, or suicide, is therefore equally as wrong as murder' (Sacred Congregation for the Doctrine of the Faith: Declaration on Euthanasia). Read an online version of the Declaration on Euthanasia and write a response to the arguments it provides.

5.2 Is natural law a good approach to euthanasia?

Applying natural law

Natural law ethics has four tiers of law (see Chapter 1), where the divine law revealed by God is higher than the natural law derived from reason. For Christians, the divine law from the Bible appears to give clear guidance against the taking of life. It is for God to bring life to an end, not human beings (see page 60). In Ecclesiastes Chapter 3, it states that there is 'a time to be born and a time to die'.

In terms of the natural law, the requirement to preserve innocent life is one of the five primary precepts. This could logically lead to a secondary precept that would prohibit euthanasia. Euthanasia itself could be thought of as an apparent good that would stand in contradiction of the real good of allowing life to continue its natural and God-given course.

Although this in theory would appear quite clear, there are a couple of considerations that may complicate the answer given by natural law. Firstly, a distinction can be drawn between ordinary and extraordinary means, as is shown by the quote from the catechism below, which shows a possible secondary precept that could be drawn. There is an obligation to give all ordinary treatment such as food, water and basic medication, yet there is no obligation to continue extraordinary treatment, which may mean that those who cannot recover should not be kept indefinitely on life-support machines. It would not be wrong for someone who is terminally ill to decline extraordinary treatment. Secondly, natural law has developed the idea of double effect (see page 8). In terms of euthanasia, it is permissible for a doctor to give strong pain relief such as morphine, even though this carries a risk of ending the patient's life. Provided the intention is to relieve pain, this would be counted as a good action.

Double effect and proportionalism

In 1999, Dr David Moor was cleared by a court of murdering a seriously ill 85-year-old cancer patient who had also had a heart attack and a stroke. A dose of morphine had hastened the death of the patient. Outside court, Dr Moor said, 'All I tried to do in treating Mr Liddell was to relieve his agony, distress and suffering. This has always been my approach in treating my patients with care and compassion. Doctors who treat dying patients to relieve their pain and suffering walk a tightrope to achieve this.'

The doctrine of double effect would support the decision taken by Dr Moor in the case above. Double effect hinges on the intention behind the action; a doctor foresees that death is a possibility, but that is not the primary intention. Of course, it is difficult to assess the intention (as this would rely on reading the doctor's mind!). Proportionalists go further than this and argue that the rules of natural law can be broken if there is a significant and proportionate reason to make an exception.

In euthanasia cases, a proportionalist such as Daniel Maguire (1931–) argues that in some cases where biological life continues but personhood is greatly diminished, shortening the process of dying is not in itself wrong. This approach is condemned by the Roman Catholic Church but it is not radically different from the idea of double effect, and the issue of determining intention would also apply here.

Analyse and evaluate

Natural law provides a good approach to euthanasia because:	Natural law does not provide a good approach to euthanasia because:
Natural law is committed to the sanctity of life. Life is valuable regardless of anyone's judgement about its quality. Thus natural law avoids the potential for a slippery slope to occur when life becomes increasingly less significant.	It is overly religious and dependent on its Christian roots. Euthanasia was often practised in the ancient world prior to the dominance of Christianity. It would seem that euthanasia should be allowed nowadays given that we are in an increasingly secular society.
Linked to this, natural law prevents individuals from playing God and making decisions about the lives of others.	Natural law can be legalistic and absolutist. Each person's situation is different, but the difficulty with natural law is that it insists on a common approach.
The idea of double effect provides some helpful flexibility in an otherwise rigid system. This allows pain relief to continue despite the frailty and vulnerability of the patient.	Natural law requires that individuals continue to live even when they are in extreme pain. A utilitarian would argue that the reduction of pain and a focus on the quality of life would be better than a natural law approach.
	In addition to the rejection of quality of life, natural law does not place sufficient weight on human autonomy. This seems odd as surely the person concerned should be absolutely central to decisions about euthanasia.
	It could be argued that double effect may in some ways be euthanasia by default. It relies on us knowing the intention of the doctor. The distinction is not always easy to see between euthanasia, which natural law rejects, and causing death as a secondary effect of pain relief.

Activities

Core

1. Explain how a supporter of natural law may use the divine law to argue against euthanasia. Aim to give at least two examples.
2. How might a natural law thinker arrive at relevant secondary precepts about euthanasia?
3. Explain with examples the difference between ordinary and extraordinary means of treatment. Which is permitted? Which is not permitted?

Stretch

4. Is double effect a helpful feature of natural law's approach to euthanasia? Consider both points of view and justify your conclusion.
5. Is it fair to reject natural law because of its religious roots? Justify your answer.

Challenge

6. Research the proportionalist approach to euthanasia as demonstrated by Daniel Maguire. How does this differ from natural law? Why does the Catholic Church support natural law but reject proportionalism?

5.3 Is situation ethics a useful approach to euthanasia?

Aim

Investigate how the theory of situation ethics can be applied to the topic of euthanasia and whether it is a useful approach.

Starter

The situation ethicist Joseph Fletcher describes a chaplain's encounter with Jim, a terminally ill patient who is married with five children. In America, medical treatment is not free and is paid for by an insurance system. The pills Jim takes, which may extend his life for three years, cost $40 every three days. Jim is quoted as saying:

'The company has me insured for $100,000. It's the only insurance I have. It's all I can leave Betts and the kids. If I take the pills and live past next October, then the policy will be cancelled when it comes to renewal. If I don't take them, at least my family have some security. If I kill myself, they get even more. If I take the pills, borrow the money for them, and then the policy lapses, that will mean that they are going to be left penniless and in debt so that even the house goes. If I don't take the pills, I'm killing myself same as if I commit suicide. What would you do? How does it look to you? I want to do the right thing.'

Imagine you are the chaplain in this case. What advice would you give? How would a refusal to accept treatment compare to suicide or euthanasia?

 How can situation ethics be applied to euthanasia?

Applying situation ethics to euthanasia

Joseph Fletcher was a keen supporter of the idea of euthanasia and, in his later years, served as president of the Euthanasia Society of America. This is entirely consistent with his writings on situation ethics.

Key quote

'It is harder to justify letting someone die a slow and ugly death, dehumanised, than it is to justify helping them escape from such misery.' (Joseph Fletcher, *Humanhood: Essays in biomedical ethics*)

For Fletcher, the sanctity of life is not an absolute. Situation ethics rejects legalism in favour of asking what is the most loving thing to do. Rules such as 'do not kill' are *sophia* (general rules of wisdom) but can be broken when love demands it. Sanctity of life (see page 60) would belong in the category of *sophia*.

Situation ethics would value quality of life and autonomy over the sanctity of life. Autonomy is especially significant as 'personalism' is one of Fletcher's four principles; it is people and their welfare rather than the keeping of laws that is at the heart of ethics.

The theory is relativist in its approach — Fletcher states that 'love's decisions are made situationally, not prescriptively'. In his 1954 book *Morals and Medicine,* he argues that the patient's medical condition has to be the starting point for any decisions in medical ethics.

This is not a total endorsement of euthanasia, but a recognition that there are cases where this is the right option.

Fletcher values pragmatism – we should do whatever is likely to work. In the topic of euthanasia there may not be ideal and perfect solutions, but what can be done is to ensure the decisions that are taken are likely to lead to the lesser of the possible evils.

Situation ethics might suggest that traditional religious ethics has come to the wrong conclusion on euthanasia as it has a mistaken rules-based view of what justice is. Yet if justice is correctly understood, to end the life of someone in great pain who does not want to live any longer would not be unjust. As Fletcher says, love is justice distributed.

Tip

It is important to note that applying the ethical theory of situation ethics or natural law to euthanasia is AO1 – knowledge and understanding – not AO2. AO2 involves assessing how useful the ethical theory is as an approach to the issue of euthanasia.

Analyse and evaluate

Situation ethics provides a good approach to euthanasia because:	Situation ethics does not provide a good approach to euthanasia because:
The flexibility of situation ethics is very useful in an issue such as euthanasia. It offers general principles rather than fixed rules and this allows us to respond to complex and varying situations.	Situation ethics can be seen as quite vague. While doing the most loving thing is a good aim, there is little guidance on what this might look like in practice. This may mean that individuals differ as to what is the most loving thing.
The idea of *agape* if correctly understood is a good moral principle and puts people first. It is a clear improvement on utilitarian ideas of maximising happiness for the majority.	Like other teleological theories, situation ethics requires a prediction of future consequences. This is not always possible in complex medical cases.
Modern technology and medical knowledge means that we are better placed to know who is or is not worth treating than we might have been years ago.	Situation ethics lacks absolute boundaries and critics of euthanasia express concern about a slippery slope that may lead to an increase in euthanasia cases, particularly for vulnerable people.
Situation ethics respects the autonomy of individuals and recognises that the patient is the most significant person in the situation.	

Activities

Core

1 In what way does the idea of pragmatism help us understand how situation ethics approaches euthanasia?
2 How does situation ethics understand the concepts of sanctity of life, quality of life and autonomy?
3 What might Fletcher say to those who would want euthanasia to be available on demand for anyone, whatever the reason? Justify your answer.

Stretch

4 Look at the arguments in the table that suggest situation ethics is a good approach to euthanasia. Which of the arguments do you consider to be the strongest? Justify your answer.
5 Look at the arguments in the table that suggest situation ethics is not a good approach to euthanasia. Which of the arguments do you consider to be the strongest? Justify your answer.

Challenge

6 Research the concept of living wills. What are the legal and ethical issues around this concept?

5.4 Should people have autonomy over their own lives and decisions?

Aim

Understand the idea of autonomy and consider how important this principle is in dealing with euthanasia.

Starter

Discuss the two cases opposite, along with the case of Tony Bland (see page 59). To what extent does the concept of autonomy – the freedom to choose – come into play?

Case study 1 – Daniel James

Daniel James was a talented rugby player who played for England under-16s. During a training session at Nuneaton Rugby Club in March 2007, he broke his spine and was left paralysed from the chest down. As a former semi-professional athlete, it was difficult for Daniel to adjust to needing parents and carers to help him do everything. Having made several unsuccessful attempts to kill himself, his parents accompanied him to the Dignitas assisted-suicide clinic in Switzerland, where Daniel died on 12 September 2008. His parents defended Daniel's decision, saying he was 'an intelligent young man of sound mind' who was 'not prepared to live what he felt was a second-class existence'.

Case study 2 – Hannah Jones

In 2008, 13-year-old Hannah Jones hit the headlines. As a result of leukaemia and heart problems, Hannah had spent most of her life in and out of hospital. Her cancer was in remission, but to stand any chance of survival she required a heart transplant, constant drug treatment and then a replacement transplant within ten years. At 13, Hannah decided she didn't want to go back into hospital and have the operation. She would rather die. She appeared on several TV programmes articulately justifying her decision.

Autonomy and euthanasia

The principle of **autonomy** states that humans should be free to make decisions about their own future. It can be traced back to J.S. Mill's non-harm principle: while the government or other authority may restrict our freedom if we are about to harm someone else, they have no right to restrict our freedom with regard to ourselves. If we wish to harm ourselves, we should be permitted to do so. Likewise, Singer's preference utilitarianism argues that humans should be free to pursue their own desires and interests where possible. This autonomy includes the right to make our own decisions about our death.

Supporters of euthanasia often appeal to the idea of autonomy. It seems to be a key aspect in determining our own lives that we have the ability to determine the time and manner of our own death. It is linked to the quality of life and in cases of voluntary euthanasia is a judgement that someone makes about the type of life they are living. Jonathan Glover has suggested that external checks are also required as to someone's state of mind, specifically that the decision is reasonable and not a temporary emotional state. If someone is making the decision in a diminished mental state then they are not truly autonomous.

Key term

Autonomy Literally 'self-ruling'; the belief that we are free and able to make our own decisions

Key quote

'I must be convinced that your decision is a serious one; it must be properly thought out, not merely the result of a temporary emotional state. I must also think your decision is a reasonable one.'
(Jonathan Glover, *Causing Death and Saving Lives*)

The issue of autonomy is more complicated in cases of non-voluntary euthanasia. If the patient has given instructions about what their wishes would be if they were in such a case then arguably their autonomy is being respected. Such examples may include a DNR (do not resuscitate) notice, where a patient has indicated that they do not want CPR to be attempted if their heart stops. Other patients may make advance directives (living wills) where they state the circumstances under which they would want treatment to stop. These are legally binding in the event of someone losing capacity to make decisions about their own treatment. Some opponents of euthanasia have expressed concern about such practices, and in 2011 it was found that some hospitals had been putting 'DNR' on the notes of frail elderly patients without proper discussion with the patient or their family.

Analyse and evaluate

People should have autonomy over their own lives and decisions because:	*People should not have autonomy over their own lives and decisions because:*
Situation ethics supports the idea of autonomy. It is a key aspect of the idea of 'personalism' that we allow individuals to make decisions about what is in their own interest.	Natural law would reject the view that autonomy is the most important consideration in issues such as euthanasia. Life is viewed as God-given and preservation of life is one of the five primary precepts.
Many of the arguments against autonomy are based on a religious notion of the sanctity of life, which becomes irrelevant if God does not exist. Regardless of whether God exists or not, the idea of God is one that over 50 per cent of people in the UK do not support, so autonomy seems a more appropriate concept for a secular age.	Autonomy is not a concept that is supported by sacred texts such as the Bible. There are specific commandments against the taking of life, the idea very much being that the time of birth and death is something that is appointed by God.
	Autonomy is a very difficult concept to apply in such a traumatic and stressful time. It is very difficult for someone in extreme physical and/or mental agony to have the clarity of thought to make good decisions about the end of their life. Similarly, in non-voluntary cases, particularly those involving vulnerable people, there is a risk of decisions being made that are not in the person's best interests, as has happened on occasions with DNRs.

Activities

Core

1 Explain how the concept of autonomy may be applied to the issues of voluntary and non-voluntary euthanasia.
2 How does J.S. Mill's non-harm principle inform our discussion of autonomy?
3 What is a DNR and in what circumstances would it apply?

Stretch

4 Psychologists have shown that it often takes up to two years to adjust following a serious trauma or bereavement. How might understanding this affect the Daniel James case? Was he exercising his autonomy? Give reasons for your answer.
5 Hannah Jones changed her mind and had a transplant several months after the events described on page 66. Using the key quote from Glover, what does this show about the difficulties of the concept of autonomy?

Challenge

6 Read Chapters 14 and 15 of Jonathan Glover's *Causing Death and Saving Lives*. Add the key ideas to your notes.

5.5 Is there a difference between acts and omissions when it comes to euthanasia?

Aim

Investigate the extent to which there may be a difference between an act that causes death and an omission that leads to the end of life.

Starter

Research the Hippocratic Oath (mentioned on page 59). What do doctors promise to do? What do they promise not to do? How does this apply to the topic of euthanasia?

Key terms

Active euthanasia A treatment is given that directly causes the death of the individual
Passive euthanasia A treatment is withheld and this indirectly causes the death of the individual

Acts and omissions – the traditional distinction

The commonly held wisdom suggests that an act that causes death is wrong, thus **active euthanasia**, whether by lethal injection or by switching off a machine, is held to be wrong by those who oppose euthanasia. **Passive euthanasia**, which involves omissions such as withdrawing a medical treatment or, as in the case of Tony Bland, a feeding tube, is often viewed as trickier. In these cases where it is clear that the patient will not recover, this may be viewed as simply allowing the person to die and this may not always be morally wrong.

Challenging thinking on acts and omissions: James Rachels

American philosopher James Rachels (1941–2003) provides a thought experiment to suggest that the distinction between actively killing and passively letting someone die may not be helpful:

● Case 1: Smith is legal guardian for his nephew and will inherit a fortune if his young nephew dies before his eighteenth birthday. (The nephew's parents have died and left the money in trust for the boy.) Smith makes plans to kill his nephew. One evening he drowns the boy in the bath and arranges the scene to look like an accident. The nephew's death is an 'act' of Smith.

● Case 2: Jones is also legal guardian for his nephew and will inherit a fortune if his young nephew dies before his eighteenth birthday. (The nephew's parents have died and left the money in trust for the boy.) Jones resents his nephew but would never intentionally harm him. As he enters the bathroom, he sees his nephew slip and hit his head on the bath and slowly drown. He watches and does nothing to save the boy. The nephew's death is an 'omission'; Jones could have saved him.

In using this as an analogy for euthanasia, the commonly held view of acts and omissions says that Smith is more guilty than Jones – thus an act is worse than an omission. Yet Rachels disputes this. He argues that both cases are equally bad and when we consider the issue of euthanasia, a passive euthanasia that operates by omission may even be more cruel, as death may take longer. In the Tony Bland case, the removal of the feeding tube meant that death did not occur until 10 days later.

Peter Singer has also challenged the distinction between acts and omissions by arguing that it is not always clear cut. The removal of Tony Bland's feeding tube, or the turning of the dial that stops the nutrients, is in some senses an action even if the removal of food is an omission. It is not totally clear whether his death is an act or an omission.

Ethical theories on acts and omissions

As with other absolutist and deontological theories, natural law would draw a distinction between acts and omissions. Key to this theory is the intention of the agent who takes action. While double effect may allow an act that leads to death, this is only in the context of this being an unintended consequence. The primary action is to relieve pain.

As with other relativist and teleological theories, situation ethics does not draw a great distinction between acts and omissions. It is pragmatic in its approach. The consequences are the most significant aspect in ethics and the outcome does not significantly change whether someone's life is ended by an action or by an omission. Their pain is relieved either way. If anything, an act that leads to death may be quicker and kinder.

Analyse and evaluate

There is a significant distinction between acts and omissions when it comes to euthanasia	*There is no significant difference between acts and omissions when it comes to euthanasia*
For natural law thinkers, actions matter. Preserving innocent life rules out acts that directly lead to death, although the idea of double effect allows that some actions may lead to the death of an individual.	Situation ethics challenges the distinction between acts and omissions. There are cases where *agape* requires the compassionate response of helping someone to end their life; whether this is by an act or an omission is not morally significant.
The distinction between acts and omissions takes seriously the issue of moral agency. If we were to allow active euthanasia, we would need doctors and other medical professionals to carry this out. This would conflict with the Hippocratic Oath and cause anxieties for those physicians who are involved.	A teleological approach that focuses on reducing pain and suffering would favour euthanasia by whichever method was most helpful in alleviating suffering.
	One practical difficulty is that withdrawal of treatment is often a lengthy process and leads to medical resources being allocated to those who will not recover. While it sounds harsh, allowing active euthanasia could speed up the inevitable process, thus freeing resources to focus on those who may recover.
	The idea of double effect is complex and not entirely coherent. If the negative consequence is foreseen then how can it truly be unintended?

Activities

Core

1 What is the difference between active and passive euthanasia?

2 How would a natural law thinker approach the issue of acts and omissions?

3 How would a situation ethicist approach the issue of acts and omissions?

Stretch

4 Write a paragraph evaluating James Rachels' thought experiment. Is there a significant difference between Smith and Jones? How good is the analogy he uses?

5 Look at the arguments in the table for and against the idea that there is a difference between acts and omissions. Which argument do you find most convincing? Justify your answer.

Challenge

6 The utilitarian Peter Singer and his colleague Helga Kuhse have written widely on the topic of euthanasia. Find out more about their views on these issues.

5.6 The Big Debate: Should active euthanasia be permitted?

 Aim

Draw together everything you have discussed in this chapter and use it to form a case either for or against the laws on active euthanasia. When you have heard both sides of the case, you decide the outcome.

 Starter

Without looking at your notes, can you explain or define the following terms: sanctity of life; quality of life; voluntary euthanasia; non-voluntary euthanasia; autonomy; active euthanasia; passive euthanasia; acts and omissions; double effect. At the end of the task, check your understanding by comparing what you have written against your notes or this textbook.

Preparing the case

Can a civilised society keep people alive against their will or is it a mark of a civilised society that we possess a belief in the sanctity and value of life?

The case for the prosecution

The law should be changed

Evidence for a change in the law surrounding euthanasia might include the following thinkers or ideas:

> **Ideas of quality of life and autonomy:** It could be argued that these matter far more than the ideas of sanctity of life, particularly in a modern, less religious age.

> **Joseph Fletcher:** Keeping someone alive against their will when they are in extreme pain cannot be the most loving thing to do.

> **Peter Singer:** In my quality of life commands, I place great value on people making their own decisions on life and death. Equally, where they cannot, those closest to them should be able to make such decisions.

> **James Rachels:** My thought experiment about acts and omissions would challenge the idea that there is something worse about active euthanasia. Passive euthanasia or allowing death by omission can, in some cases, make matters worse.

The case for the defence

The law should not be changed

Evidence for not changing the law surrounding euthanasia might include the following thinkers/ideas:

Ideas about sanctity of life: There is something special and significant about human life. We ought not to make decisions about other people's lives, particularly if we believe that life is God-given.

Thomas Aquinas: Preserving life is one of the five primary precepts; these are principles that we can work out rationally. Humans can't flourish or please God if we ignore such a key rule.

Disability-rights pressure groups: There are big concerns about the potential for a slippery slope. By allowing euthanasia, particularly where relatives make decisions on behalf of someone else, we open the door to vulnerable people feeling they are a burden on society.

I'll see you in court

You can work through the process below individually either verbally or in written form (sometimes verbalising thoughts is the first step to being able to write them down), or you could work through the activities as a group or class, debating and reaching a verdict.

The judge opens the case: What is the current legal position on euthanasia? What are the different forms of euthanasia? How do they differ? What important issues might need to be considered?

↓

The case for the prosecution is presented: The law should be changed. What are the key arguments in favour of changing the law? What key evidence would be presented?

↓

Defence cross-examination: What are the issues arising from this evidence? What counterarguments can be brought forward?

↓

The case for the defence is presented: The law should not be changed. What are the key arguments against changing the law? What key evidence would be presented?

Prosecution cross-examination: What are the issues arising from this evidence? What counterarguments can be brought forward?

↓

Closing speeches: What is the key piece of evidence for the prosecution case?
What is the key piece of evidence for the defence case?

↓

Jury decision: What conclusion do you reach? Why? (If you are doing this exercise as a class/group, you can take a vote.)

Activities

Core

1 Create a large concept map that outlines the case in favour of active euthanasia.

2 Create a large concept map that outlines the case against active euthanasia.

3 Write a speech to use in the court case – select one of the arguments or scholars. Make your speech persuasive by adding justified reasons and examples to support your view.

Stretch

4 Write questions to ask the defence and prosecution witnesses. Make them as tricky as possible.

5 Think about possible answers to your questions – how could you respond and challenge the witness further? (This is developing the skill of critical analysis found in AO2 Level 6.)

Challenge

6 Write a conclusion for this debate. Did you or your class decide that active euthanasia should be permitted? Which evidence did you find most persuasive and why? Are there any doubts left? If so, what are the doubts and why were they not answered in the case? Can you think of ways to answer those doubts now?

Wrap up

QUIZ

1 What does the word euthanasia literally mean?

2 What is the term that describes withholding treatment and in doing so indirectly causing the death of the individual?

3 Which utilitarian philosopher suggests five quality of life commandments?

4 Why is the Hippocratic Oath significant for this topic?

5 Give examples of the difference between ordinary and extraordinary means.

6 Which key thinker once served as president of the Euthanasia Society of America?

7 What is meant by the slippery slope argument?

8 Which ethical theory views life as intrinsically valuable?

9 What might be shown by biblical texts such as Exodus 20:13 and Job 1:21?

10 What does the acronym PVS stand for?

GET READY

Summarising

1 Create a set of flash cards for the technical terms that you have come across during the lessons in this chapter and your independent study. Test yourself on the definitions.

2 Building the AO1: Write a 100-word summary for a) natural law and b) situation ethics, showing how they apply to euthanasia. Aim to be succinct and provide three or four ideas for each.

Linking

3 AO2 links: This topic is an excellent chance to review past topics on the ethical theories. Look through your notes on the strengths and weaknesses of both natural law and situation ethics and make a list of which ones might apply to euthanasia. Practise writing a few paragraphs applying these points.

Applying

4   Make a concept map on paper or use an online concept-mapping tool such as Coggle to gain an overview of this topic.

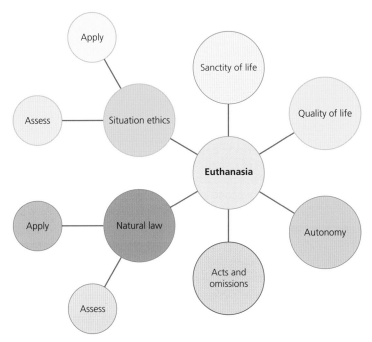

5   Plan and paragraph (P&P) essay planning: Draw two shapes on to a blank piece of paper, as shown below. In the first one, write a plan for an essay asking you whether natural law or situation ethics provides a better approach to euthanasia.

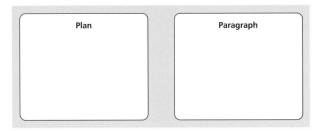

In the second shape, write one of the paragraphs in full. If you can write one good paragraph, there is no reason why you cannot write a good essay. Essays are, after all, a collection of paragraphs.

Debate

6   'The quality of life is far more important than the sanctity of life.'
Discuss this in small groups and make a note of the points raised. Add them to your notes.

Going further

7   Which of the two ethical theories you have studied provides the better approach to euthanasia? Give reasons for your answer.

CHECKLIST

I know, understand and can ...

☐   explain in detail the ideas of sanctity of life and quality of life

☐   explain what is meant by voluntary and non-voluntary euthanasia

☐   explain and assess how well the theory of natural law addresses euthanasia

☐   explain and assess how well the theory of situation ethics addresses euthanasia

☐   consider whether the sanctity of life is important in twenty-first-century ethics

☐   assess whether a person should have complete control and autonomy over their own life and death

☐   consider the moral significance of acting to end a life or omitting to act to save a life.

Get practising

Ask the expert

'I struggle with AO2. My teacher has told me to develop my points in more depth but I am at a loss to know what he means. The structure I use worked well at GCSE so I'm not sure why it doesn't work at A level.' – Ruqayya

Ruqayya's paragraph

Situation ethics has a number of weaknesses when it is applied to euthanasia. First it is vague as it does not show us what love requires in a situation. It also has difficulties because it is difficult to know what results will occur from the decision as situation ethics requires us to predict the future and we often don't know which decision will result in the most loving outcome until after we have made the decision. Situation ethics is a religious theory and this is also a weakness as we are now in a more secular society and so a religious theory may not be the best way of making moral decisions with regard to euthanasia.

Ruqayya is trying to do too much in one paragraph. There are three separate points, each of which could be its own paragraph. This would allow the point to be unpacked and explained in detail and some discussion/evaluation as to how strong the argument is. The structure that serves people fairly well at GCSE, of listing points for and points against and only really commenting on the strength of arguments in the conclusion, is not likely to lead to high marks for AO2 at A level. Lily's paragraph below uses the PEACE technique to fully unpack her point.

Give PEACE a chance

There are a number of different ways of writing AO2-led paragraphs. One technique is to use the acronym PEACE:

P **Point**: A clear AO2 statement of an argument relevant to the question.

E **Explain**: The point is developed – why is it important? Remember that you are writing for the 'educated alien'.

A **Assess**: An evaluation/consideration of how strong the initial point is (weigh the argument). And/or:

C **Counterargument**: A response that a critic might make to the initial point.

E **Evaluative judgement**: Reach an intermediate conclusion based on the initial point.

Lily's paragraph

A key reason why situation ethics may not be an effective approach to euthanasia is that the idea of *agape* love is held to be vague. It is quite possible that two different people may look at an identical situation, such as a person terminally ill with cancer, and form opposite views about what the most loving thing to do is, whether that be euthanasia or stronger pain relief, hence it is often unclear what the most loving thing is.

Point

Explain

This is a strong argument as for an ethical theory to be considered effective, it surely has to give a clear answer. Yet while the vagueness may be true in a few of the most complex cases, this is certainly not always the case. In most cases it seems very clear what love requires; it requires a compassionate end to suffering and thus love is actually quite clear. Hence the criticism that situation ethics may be vague is not particularly effective because there is clarity in the vast majority of cases.

Asse[ss]

Counterargument

Evaluative judgement

CHAPTER 6

Business ethics

▲ Workers in sweat shops work 14–16-hour shifts, earning just over half the money they need for food, housing and other essentials. Some of the workers are children. Most of the garments produced are sold in Europe and North America

▲ Sue works in the shop regularly and knows that Mr Jones' dementia means he will not check his change. She makes an extra £20 each week from his visits

▲ Mike Ashley, Director of Sports Direct. A report in 2016 by MPs stated 'Sports Direct staff not treated as humans'

Big picture

Our culture values making money, but are there ethical limits to how this should be done? Is all fair in business or should there be moral rules that govern how businesses behave?

Engage

Consider the situations below:

1   Employment law in Bangladesh allows the practices shown in the top photograph. Do you agree that it makes sense for a British business to save money by getting clothes made in Bangladesh?

2   Mr Jones is very rich and Sue is struggling to pay her bills. Are her actions still wrong? Justify your answer.

3   Find out about what was happening at the Sports Direct warehouse in 2016. What surprises you? The business has since made significant improvements to workers' conditions.

The specification

Content	Key knowledge
Key ideas of business ethics, including: • corporate social responsibility • whistleblowing • good ethics is good business • globalisation	• What it is (that a business has responsibility towards the community and environment) and its application to stakeholders, such as employees, customers, the local community, the country as whole and governments • What it is (that an employee discloses wrongdoing to the employer or the public) and its application to the contract between employee and employer • What it is (that good business decisions are good ethical decisions) and its application to shareholders and profit-making • What it is (that around the world economies, industries, markets, cultures and policy-making is integrated) and its impact on stakeholders

Learners should have the opportunity to discuss issues raised by these areas of business ethics, including:
• the application of Kantian ethics and utilitarianism to business ethics
• whether or not the concept of corporate social responsibility is nothing more than 'hypocritical window-dressing' covering the greed of a business intent on making profits
• whether or not human beings can flourish in the context of capitalism and consumerism
• whether globalisation encourages or discourages the pursuit of good ethics as the foundation of good business.

6.1 What are the key issues in business ethics?

Aim

Learn the key ideas affecting the topic of business ethics in the modern day.

Starter

Sanjeev felt sure he stood a good chance of getting the job of Deputy Head. He has far more experience than Alison and he knows that her application went in two days late. He was disappointed to learn that she had got the job and suspected the fact that she was the Head's partner may have been significant. He wants to tackle the issue but a friend reminds him how the Head of Science 'disappeared' last year after a row with the Head. What ethical issues are there here? What should Sanjeev do?

Key term

Corporate social responsibility The idea that a business has responsibilities towards the community and environment (all stakeholders)

Corporate social responsibility

The idea of **corporate social responsibility** is at the heart of business ethics. This goes beyond just obeying the law and suggests that businesses have ethical responsibilities towards their employees, the community and the environment. They are responsible not just to their shareholders (those who own or invest money in the business) but also to their stakeholders. A stakeholder is defined as 'an individual or group which either is harmed or benefits from the corporation OR whose rights can be violated, or have to be respected, by the business' (Crane and Matten, *Business Ethics*).

A business might exercise corporate social responsibility in a number of ways, for example investing in staff wellbeing activities such as yoga, sponsoring a youth football team, donating prizes for a charity draw, aiming to recycle more of the water that it uses.

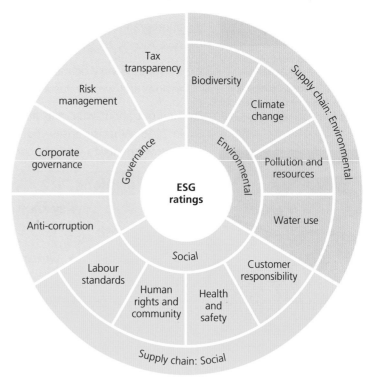

▲ The FTSE4Good Index shows a number of measures that businesses can be judged on in order to establish how responsible they are (their ESG rating)

Whistleblowing

The case of Sanjeev (see the Starter box) may lead to an act of **whistleblowing**. Whistleblowing in business refers to the practice of an employee drawing attention to unethical or illegal activity taking place within a business. They may do this internally by raising it confidentially with senior staff within the business or more publicly by alerting the media or authorities to what is happening within the business. Many businesses have policies and procedures to allow the former to take place. In Sanjeev's case, the school governors or the local authority could be contacted.

Key terms

Whistleblowing An employee discloses unethical or illegal business practices to the employer or the public

A whistleblower may draw attention to various things, such as:

- tax avoidance within a business
- environmental issues that the company wishes to hide
- cheating on tests or exams
- discrimination or bias in recruitment or promotion procedures.

Although in theory whistleblowers have legal protection, the reality is that often there is a great cost in raising concerns; this may be loss of friendships, poor treatment subsequently from managers, and on occasions the loss of their job.

The social responsibility of business

 Meet the thinker

Milton Friedman was an American economist whose idea of monetarism with its decrease in government rules and regulations for business has proved very influential on British and American thinking. In 'The Social Responsibility of Business is to increase its profits' he argues against corporate social responsibility.

◀ Milton Friedman (1912–2006)

Friedman argues that suggesting businesses should have responsibilities is a mistake. This would lead to socialism rather than capitalism. A business is not like a person and cannot have responsibilities.

Suggesting that a business should have ethical responsibilities in addition to the law distracts the business from its core purpose, which is to make money. Friedman argues that it is a mistake to imply that the pursuit of profit is in some way immoral.

If the business is successful in making money then there may be benefits to the community as employees have some money and are able to use it for good. There is nothing to stop individual executives or employees giving part of their wages to charity or volunteering in the community in their own time, but as representatives of the company as a whole this distracts from the pursuit of profit. If money is taken from shareholders to fund social responsibility projects, this is like stealing from the company!

Activities

Core

1. What is corporate social responsibility? Give some examples to illustrate your answer.
2. What are the two different types of whistleblowing? Give an example of each.
3. According to Milton Friedman, why is it wrong for businesses to pursue corporate social responsibility?

Stretch

4. Choose a well-known business. Write a paragraph identifying who the stakeholders of the business are. What responsibilities might the business have to each of these stakeholders?
5. 'It is always right to tell the truth.' Explain why things may not be so straightforward in whistleblowing cases. In terms of whistleblowing, do you agree with the quote? Give reasons for your answer.

Challenge

6. Milton Friedman's article is widely available online. Read it and add to your notes on this key thinker.

6.2 How helpful is a utilitarian approach to business ethics?

Aim

Investigate how utilitarianism can be applied to business ethics and consider whether it is an effective approach.

Starter

1 Spend 5 minutes writing down what you already know about utilitarianism. The following words should feature in your notes: Bentham; Mill; act; rule; hedonic calculus.

2 The CEO of Waterfield's Widgets faces a decision. It is possible to close the UK factory, which provides 400 jobs in a poorer area of the city, and open up a new factory in the Philippines where wages are much lower and there is less business regulation. This would enable the widgets to be produced much cheaper. The resulting saving could be a huge profit for the company and/or be passed on to customers by lowering the price of each item. What are the pros and cons involved in this decision? What are the ethical issues?

Applying utilitarianism to business ethics

At a simple level, many businesses operate by almost a utilitarian approach in day-to-day decision-making, using something called a cost–benefit analysis. Here, the financial, human and environmental costs of an action are given a value, as are the benefits of the action, and the business then makes its decision accordingly. This case-by-case decision-making is similar to act utilitarianism.

In applying Bentham's act utilitarianism there is a danger that the focus on pleasure and pain could be quite narrow and lead to shallow decision-making that may ignore people's rights. Mill has a more subtle understanding of what the 'greatest good' means and appeals to the idea of higher and lower pleasures; happiness is much broader than simple pleasure vs pain.

Act utilitarianism allows a business some flexibility. Business A might close a factory in the UK to send jobs abroad, but Business B may make a different decision because the negative press coverage of doing this would be likely to lead to loss of sales. However, being unsure what a business is likely to do may lead to uncertainty and a lack of confidence among investors and customers. A more rule-based utilitarianism, where a company adopts certain values or principles by which it operates, may lead to more consistency.

Tip

If a question asks you to apply utilitarianism, remember that there are different forms of utilitarianism. Be precise when answering the question – don't just suggest that all utilitarians are looking for pleasure/greater good.

Analyse and evaluate

Defending a utilitarian view	Difficulties with a utilitarian view
Businesses are results-driven. As a teleological ethical theory, utilitarianism ensures that the focus is on achieving the best outcome.	Act utilitarianism is very time-consuming in the fast-paced business world. If we consider every single possible effect on utility and all possible consequences, decision-making becomes a very complicated and lengthy process.
Act utilitarianism in particular gives flexibility to different situations. Each situation that a business faces is likely to be unique and it may not be appropriate to have an ethical theory that is rule-based.	Utilitarianism has no concept of rights and does not value justice (unless injustice can be shown to affect overall utility!). Bentham famously referred to belief in human rights as 'nonsense on stilts'. Hence we are left with the feeling that a utilitarian could allow things that many of us would regard as unethical in order to reach an end.
Bentham's utilitarianism is hedonistic, suggesting that humans are motivated entirely by pain and pleasure. Advertisers use this principle of appealing to our desires or playing on our fears in selling products; this suggests Bentham is not wrong about our motives.	It is not clear that the objectivity and impartiality utilitarianism promises can be achieved. Experience of pleasure and pain and our ideas of greater good are often subjective. We may see a situation very differently from how someone else views it.
Utilitarianism depersonalises issues. Mill refers to the competent judge (page 46); Singer refers to the impartial observer (page 52). This means that personal bias is laid aside and we are hopefully able to look at issues objectively.	It is also difficult to compare the different 'goods' that may or may not be achieved by any given decision. An environmental benefit, a wage rise, and an improvement in working conditions would all be measured in different ways.

 Tip

In addition to the points listed on this page, consider the general strengths and weaknesses of utilitarianism (Chapter 4). Ask yourself which might equally apply when considering business.

Activities

Core

1 What is a cost–benefit analysis? What would need to be considered?

2 How might Bentham and Mill differ when approaching business ethics?

3 Which of the advantages of utilitarianism do you think is most important? Which of the disadvantages?

Stretch

4 Look again at the second question in the Starter activity. What would a cost–benefit analysis look like? Adopt a utilitarian perspective and make a decision. Try to write one or two paragraphs justifying your decision.

5 Choose two of the AO2 points listed in the table above. Practise transforming these points into paragraphs fully explaining the idea, perhaps suggesting a counterargument and reaching a conclusion.

Challenge

6 Research Peter Singer's preference utilitarianism if you have not already done so (see Stretch activity, page 51). How might this apply to the issues raised on this page, particularly with regard to treatment of the developing world?

6.3 How helpful is a Kantian approach to business ethics?

Aim

Learn how Kantian ethics applies to business and consider how effective this approach is.

Starter

1 Spend 5 minutes writing down what you already know about Kantian ethics. The following words should feature in your notes: good will, duty, categorical imperative, universal law, persons as ends.

2 The managing director of Dean's Delicious Burgers needs greater flexibility in staffing. By moving to zero-hours contracts, where workers do not have fixed or guaranteed hours but can be given extra shifts when needed, she will be able to cope with busy weeks, quiet weeks and those unexpected times when a member of staff is sick or leaves. It also means, however, that people do not have regular shifts, which can lead to there being too many staff when it is known that the period will be quiet. What are the advantages and disadvantages for those concerned? What ethical issues might be raised?

Applying Kantian ethics

Kantian ethics is based on the idea of duty: that we as moral agents owe certain things to those we come into contact with, regardless of our inclination or whether we will benefit from the action in question. Kant argues that we can work out what our moral duty is by finding categorical imperatives based on what can be universalised and based on our treatment of persons. For Kant, our duty takes precedence over making money. This affects both the employer, who would have a duty to pay a fair wage, as well as the employee, who would have a duty not to take excessive breaks or overclaim on expenses as this would be dishonest and violate the universal law test.

Motive is also important to Kant. He gives the example of a shopkeeper who treats customers well because it is good for business, thus acting in accordance with duty. But this is not a purely good act as the motive is wrong. A shopkeeper who acts out of duty – their motive is to do the right thing – would be better.

Perhaps more significant is the requirement to treat persons – employees, customers, and even competitors – as an end rather than a means to an end. This type of thinking takes corporate social responsibility seriously and leads to the idea of rights; it has been influential in employment law. All stakeholders need to be considered, not just those who own the business. For example, if a business is using child labour somewhere in its supply chain then those children are being treated as a means to an end, and various rights, including the right to an education, are being violated.

Kantian ethics puts a great value on honesty. This would affect claims that a business makes in its advertising and the extent to which it communicates with its workers if there are financial difficulties that may lead to job losses. In most cases, whistleblowing could be supported where there are ethical concerns as, in Kantian ethics, the truth needs to be told. Although employees have a duty to their company, they also have wider ethical responsibilities.

John Rawls

One modern philosopher who has used Kantian principles and developed an ethic based on rights and justice is John Rawls (1921–2002). Rawls defines justice as fairness and argues that equality should be understood as equality of opportunity rather than equity. To illustrate what he means by fairness, Rawls asks us to imagine that before we are born we stand behind a 'veil of ignorance', not knowing what our situation in life will be: not knowing our gender, our race, whether we will be disabled, able-bodied, rich or poor. If this were the case, we would agree the following two rules in order to ensure justice (fairness) occurred:

1 Each person to have equal access to basic rights and liberties.
2 Social and economic inequalities to be arranged so that they:
    a have the greatest benefit for the disadvantaged (e.g. less tax for the poor)
    b give equal opportunity for the disadvantaged to achieve high office and position on merit.

Rawls argues that the wealthy should expect to pay more tax to address the inequality in society.

Analyse and evaluate

Defending a Kantian view	Difficulties with a Kantian view
The principle of universal law requires that we are consistent in our ethical decision-making. This is important as it enables us to treat others equally and builds trust, ensuring that people know what to expect from us.	Kantian ethics is a very abstract theory that does not always translate well to practical real-world situations. For instance, it is unrealistic and naïve to think that a business should not consider profit at all in order to pursue an ethical goal. Businesses cannot survive without profit.
The principle of treating others as ends not as a means to an end is important in ensuring that those whom we deal with, whether employees or customers, are not treated just as data or numbers.	The principle of universal law is not useful in business ethics. Each situation encountered is unique and different, so insisting that an action be able to be applied universally is not helpful.
Kant's focus on the importance of motives ensures that corporate social responsibility is genuine and not just an act or marketing ploy to attract customers.	Focusing on motive is difficult as motives cannot be proved. In Kant's example of the shopkeeper (page 80), whether the shopkeeper is 'acting out of duty' or merely 'in accordance with duty' is indistinguishable from the outside and is known only by the shopkeeper.
	There are numerous stakeholders in business that we may have duties to, so there are inevitably times when we have conflicting duties. A key difficulty of Kantian ethics is conflicting duties. We may not be able to satisfy everyone.

Activities

Core

1 What does it mean to treat someone as a means to an end? Give an example related to business ethics.
2 What are Kant's views about telling the truth? How does this apply to whistleblowing?
3 Which of the advantages of Kantian ethics is the most important? Which of the disadvantages of Kantian ethics is most important? Give a reason for your answer.

Stretch

4 Research the gig economy. What ethical issues does it raise for employees? What do you think Kant would make of such employment practices?

5 Choose two of the AO2 points listed in the table above. Practise transforming these points into paragraphs fully explaining the idea, perhaps suggesting a counterargument and reaching a conclusion.

Challenge

6 Research the Rawls–Nozick debate on justice. One of the main issues surrounds the wages of basketball player Wilt Chamberlain and whether it is fair for him to pay so much tax. Which of the thinkers do you agree with? Give a reason for your answer.

6.4 Does globalisation encourage ethical action?

Aim

Learn about globalisation and how this affects the topic of business ethics.

Starter

Use sticky notes to define individual differences in how Fred and Sasha below are able to approach business. What are their markets? What is their competition? How quickly can things happen? How do they communicate?

▲ Farmer Fred (18th century)   ▲ CEO Sasha (present day)

Key term

Globalisation The integration of economies, industries, markets, cultures and policymaking around the world

Globalisation

Globalisation is the integration and connection of economies, industries and governments around the world. In metaphorical terms it may be said that the world is getting smaller. Globalisation recognises that the modern world in which business occurs is vastly different even from the world of 50 years ago. The main impact is that business and social interaction are not necessarily restricted to one territory or geographical area. According to Crane and Matten, this can be seen in two main ways:

- **Technological:** Communication and travel have meant that businesses can reach further and trade more widely. International trade can be done in days in terms of movement of goods and paid for in seconds over the internet, as opposed to taking months by boat.
- **Political:** It is almost impossible for countries to be completely self-sufficient; each needs goods produced by others. This means that economic issues in one country often affect other countries. Countries cannot work or set laws in isolation.

Globalisation and ethics

It has been suggested that globalisation completely changes the topic of business ethics and brings dilemmas and benefits that previous generations had no need to consider. Large companies known as multinational corporations (MNCs), which operate over many different countries, have become increasingly powerful: a MNC can often turn over more money than a small country's whole economy, and it has been estimated that two-thirds of all world trade is carried out by MNCs. There are concerns that such companies are able to use their influence to seek out cheap labour in less developed countries and damage the environment by working in countries where environmental laws are more relaxed.

Crane and Matten suggest three areas where globalisation is relevant to business ethics:

1. **Cultural issues:** Difficulties can be caused due to different cultural beliefs and attitudes. European businesses have different attitudes to gender equality from some Middle Eastern countries. Europeans regard child labour as completely unethical, whereas some Asian countries may take a very different view. There are also differences in terms of loyalty. In China, for instance, loyalty is valued greatly and businesses may be less likely to sack employees just because times are hard. Another cultural concern is that globalisation is contributing to a loss of local identity and culture, with every town centre whether in Beijing or Brighton having largely the same shops and brands.

2. **Legal issues:** Laws are geographically limited, for example UK law applies only in the UK. By operating in a multinational context, companies are able to exploit this by ensuring that something that would be illegal in one country is done in a different country where it is not illegal.

For example, a company in the UK is required to pay minimum wage and abide by maximum working hours, but these laws do not apply if the work is done in Bangladesh. There are also some aspects of business, such as financial markets and content on the internet, that is not easily controlled by national borders.

3 **Accountability issues:** Whereas a company that is based in one country is clearly accountable to the laws and governance of that country, it is difficult to see how an MNC can be held accountable for its actions. Some companies have become so large and powerful that there is no real accountability outside of the company itself.

Analyse and evaluate

Globalisation discourages ethical action because:	*Globalisation encourages ethical action because:*
Globalisation has been described as producing a 'race to the bottom' in terms of wages, workers' rights and environmental standards. Corporations are keen to cut costs and consumers are keen to have goods as cheaply as possible. Globalisation makes this possible by exploiting people and their environments. This was seen very tragically in the 2013 Rana Plaza disaster, where over 1000 people were killed when a garment factory collapsed due to employers ignoring the hazardous working conditions.	'Globalisation has reduced the number of extreme poor in India by 200 million and in China by 300 million since 1990' (Jeffrey Sachs, *The End of Poverty*). A utilitarian may point to the benefits of globalisation as millions of people in developing countries have been lifted out of poverty.
In many countries the gap between rich and poor is growing. While globalisation benefits some people, many of the poorest in society have become even more badly off.	The technological advances in communication, particularly around the internet and social media, mean that it is harder for companies to hide unethical practices. Whistleblowers can tweet within seconds; TV news can inform millions about what is happening. Although Kant might argue that this shouldn't be a company's motive in acting morally, in practice worries about reputation prevent much unethical behaviour.
A Kantian may have real concerns about the effects of globalisation on persons. A multinational corporation is in effect treating those in the developing world as a means to an end, and in closing factories in the USA or Europe is treating these workers as a means to an end as well.	
The rise of globalisation causes almost a neo-colonialism, where the standards and values of the developed western world are gradually imposed and/or produce tension with indigenous cultures.	

Activities

Core

1 What is meant by globalisation?
2 What are some of the ethical issues that are raised by globalisation?
3 Is globalisation a good or bad thing for ethics? Give a developed reason for your answer.

Stretch

4 Research the 2013 Rana Plaza disaster. How does it relate to the concerns identified in this chapter?

5 How might a utilitarian and a Kantian view the issues around globalisation? Write a paragraph on each one.

Challenge

6 Globalisation is about both economic and environmental issues. Find out about the environmentalist Arne Næss. What are his ideas? How would they slow down the effects of globalisation? Do you think they would work?

6.5 Can people flourish in a capitalist, consumerist society?

Aim

Investigate whether our current capitalist society focused on the pursuit of money and things is good for us as human beings.

Starter

Using the internet, research the Occupy Wall Street and Occupy London protests. What were the protestors' main concerns?

▲ A slogan is unveiled at the Occupy London protests

Key terms

Capitalism An economic system based on private ownership and free trade rather than government intervention
Consumerism A belief in the importance of acquiring material things

Political systems

Capitalism is an economic system where the means of production (how things are made and sold) are owned by private individuals/businesses. The government aims to do less centrally and allows businesses to provide services, to trade freely and to make a profit doing so. Socialism views social goods as more important than individual businesses making profits. Socialism has more direct government involvement and many of the means of production are publicly owned (shared by society). Communism/Marxism is a very extreme form of socialism that aims to exercise total control over the economy. The main differences between capitalism and socialism are explained in the table.

Capitalism	Socialism
Private ownership	Public ownership
De-regulation of business	Higher business regulation
Freedom of choice	Some choice restricted
Lower taxes – reduced public services	Higher taxes – more public services
Law of supply and demand	

Capitalism and Adam Smith

Most western democracies operate by the principles of capitalism. The philosopher and economist Adam Smith (1723–90) is viewed as one of the key founders of the idea of capitalism. Smith argues that individuals make moral decisions based upon their own self-interest, a position known as ethical egoism, but this generally works for the good of all people despite capitalism being based largely on competition. One key economic principle that comes from Smith is the law of supply and demand: the amount of goods available will determine how much a business can charge; the number of workers trained to do a job will determine how much their labour is worth.

Smith argues that businesses need to pay attention to how efficiently they can produce things. The division of labour makes factory production more efficient. Instead of one person doing all the stages of the manufacturing process, a 'conveyer belt'-type system that splits production into stages is more efficient, even if it is more boring for the workers. It is this division of labour that Karl Marx (1818–83) criticises when he argues that people have become alienated from their work.

Analyse and evaluate

Why humans cannot flourish in a capitalist, consumerist society	Why capitalism enables humans to flourish
Capitalism is based on competition, which means that economically there are winners and losers. It can be said to bring out the worst in people given that, as Smith admits, we operate out of self-interest.	Societies that have embraced capitalism have tended to grow economically, with the result that, on average, people in those countries are richer.
Karl Marx famously criticised the capitalism of his day after seeing rich factory owners oppressing their workers. Making massive profits but paying your workers poorly does not allow them to flourish. He would not approve of how some modern companies give million-pound salaries to the CEO but pay workers the minimum wage.	Although not a utilitarian as such, Smith's ideas do satisfy utilitarian criteria and lead to the greater good and happiness of the majority.
Religious teaching opposes the idea that we are merely consumers focused on gaining material goods. Christians believe that humans are made in the image of God and have higher purposes. Many Christians point to the teachings of Jesus with his warnings about money, such as in the story of the Rich Young Ruler. Capitalism also often leads to damage to the environment, which Christians believe is a gift given by God.	The Parable of the Talents may reinforce the idea of using abilities to make money in competition with others. The one who makes the most is praised by Jesus.
In Kantian ethics it could be argued that the word 'consumer' implies a means-to-an-end relationship. Kant believes that humans are rational, autonomous and possess dignity. Reducing us to consumers misses this.	

Activities

Core

1   What is the key difference between capitalism and socialism?
2   Explain what is meant by the law of supply and demand. Give an example.
3   How do Smith and Marx differ on the division of labour?

Stretch

4   Use the information on this page to produce an essay plan for a question on whether humans can flourish in a capitalist society. Write out your conclusion in full.

5   Find out more about Marx's criticism of capitalist society. What does he think is the way to solve the problems of capitalism?

Challenge

6   Smith's position is known as ethical egoism. Find out more about this. In what ways is it similar to utilitarianism? What are the differences?

6.6 Is it true that good ethics is good business?

Aim

Investigate the view that good business decisions are good ethical decisions.

Starter

Using your knowledge from the topic so far, add to the point made by each of the thinkers by giving a reason for their views. The word 'because' should appear somewhere in each of your sentences.

No, ethics is not relevant to business.

Yes, good ethics IS good business.

No, good ethics is more important than good business.

▲ Milton Friedman (1912–2006) Adam Smith (1723–1790) Immanuel Kant (1724–1804)

Smith on the relationship between ethics and business

The idea that good ethics is good business is a fair summary of the views of Adam Smith. Smith identifies that there are relationships in business where two things inevitably interact for the benefit of the other. The word 'symbiotic' describes this sort of relationship.

- Businesses and consumers are one sort of symbiotic relationship – businesses benefit when they treat their customers well, thus in turn making the customers more likely to return to that business.

- Likewise, a business's relationship with its employees is also symbiotic; it is an accepted truth that workers who feel appreciated and supported will typically be more loyal and hardworking, thus benefiting the business.

Thus, a wise and sensible business owner will endeavour to do the right thing as far as possible for both customers and employees, as this is likely to be beneficial in the long run. This is particularly true in the age of globalisation and social media as news of poor ethics can travel very fast, whether it is a local shop shortchanging customers or a multinational corporation using child workers as part of its supply chain overseas.

Facebook data scandal

In 2018, news broke that Facebook had allowed data from 50 million users to be used by a political consulting firm called Cambridge Analytica. Facebook had initially allowed this for academic research purposes, however this data was used to profile users and target them with adverts. It was used for this purpose by the Trump presidential campaign and, it is alleged, by the Leave campaign in the 2016 UK referendum. On the day that Facebook CEO Mark Zuckerberg testified in front of Congress, the Facebook share price lost 16 per cent of its value.

Key quote

'It is not from the benevolence of the butcher, the brewer, or the baker that we expect our dinner, but from their regard to their own self-interest.'
(Adam Smith, *The Wealth of Nations*)

France Telecom suicides

In 2019, Didier Lombard, former boss of France Telecom, and two executives were jailed for their part in a restructuring policy that was linked to 19 suicides among employees. It was the first time that a French court had recognised the crime of 'institutional harassment'. Lombard had been tasked with a major reorganisation of the company, which needed to cut 22,000 jobs and retrain 10,000 employees. Workers were deliberately transferred away from their families or given demeaning jobs in an attempt to 'encourage' them to voluntarily resign. 'I'll get them out one way or another, through the window or through the door,' Lombard was heard to tell his senior team at a meeting in 2007.

Analyse and evaluate

Good ethics is (usually) good for business because:	Good ethics is not always good for business because:
For some thinkers it does not really matter whether corporate social responsibility is genuine or not; the results are the same regardless of the motive. The economist Adam Smith (page 86) suggests that businesses have a symbiotic relationship with both their customers and their employees. Our self-interest will more than likely lead us to treat others well. It is short-sighted to overcharge customers or pay low wages, as we will harm our reputation and may ultimately make less money. As business is built on reputations and confidence, an ethical approach will pay off. It does not even matter if the motives are questionable.	Milton Friedman (page 77) would reject any link between business and ethics. While agreeing with Smith that there could be occasions when being ethical increases profits, there may be other occasions where being overly ethical could cause losses. Here the business should prioritise making money over being ethical.
Utilitarians may on most occasions support Smith in this view. The consequences of bad ethical decisions are often very great. A reputation can be ruined in seconds and it can take years for a business to recover.	Immanuel Kant would also challenge the link but for a different reason. Kant would argue that good ethics, doing our duty, is far more important than good business. Kant uses the example of a shopkeeper who always charges others fairly because he knows that this is good for business – in the way that Smith and the utilitarians might suggest. Yet Kant concludes that even this is not sufficient for the action to count as morally good. It is only if the shopkeeper does the right thing out of duty, and would continue to do so even if he lost money, that this becomes a good action. Hence the business should prioritise ethics over making money.

Activities

Core

1. What is the most important aim of business according to Friedman?
2. Why might a utilitarian argue that good ethics is good for business?
3. What point is Kant making about the honest shopkeeper?

Stretch

4. Write a paragraph summarising what Friedman, Smith and Kant may say about the link between ethics and business. Are the two concepts linked? Which is most important?
5. 'What are my customers going to get from me that they aren't going to get from someone else? Are you the cheap one, the one with good service, the ethical or bespoke one? What's your hook?' (Lord Sugar). Is being 'ethical' just another way of positioning your business? Write a paragraph justifying your answer.

Challenge

6. Do some online research about the Fairtrade movement. In what ways does this movement have ethical benefits? Does this help generate business or does it reduce the money that is made?

6.7 The Big Debate: Does it matter if corporate social responsibility is genuine?

Aim

Investigate whether it matters if ethical behaviour arises from genuine motives or not. You will consider the evidence and reach a verdict.

Starter

Eyre's Ethical Café is doing very well. Since opening in a relatively prosperous town centre filled with young professionals, its range of ethically sourced products such as Fairtrade coffee sell well; around the walls are posters explaining how sustainable and environmentally friendly the business really is. The owner is seen to cycle everywhere, although as he tells close friends it is really just clever business. He doesn't particularly care for the environment or his workers. The people of the town are very ethically aware and happy to pay a little more to take the ethical option.

The owner – the defendant – stands accused of not behaving ethically at all. What are your initial views? What might some of the thinkers you have studied on this topic have to say?

Preparing the case

Does it matter if the underlying motives of business owners are to make profits, and their corporate social responsibility is in fact just a pretense? Surely the end results are the same regardless of motive?

The case for the prosecution

The defendant is guilty of not genuinely being interested in corporate social responsibility

Evidence that motive matters might include the following thinkers and ideas:

> **Immanuel Kant:** There is a difference between acting in accordance with duty and acting out of duty. Pretending to care about ethical concerns but in reality caring more about profit is not ethical at all.

> **Corporate social responsibility:** Businesses do have wider responsibilities to their communities and all stakeholders. If the intentions are not genuine, at some point the mask will slip as what people really think will inevitably come out in their treatment of others.

> **Mr G. Reed:** I am the landlord of the Frog and Ferret pub and Mr Eyre has been heard giving derogatory views about environmental issues and workers' rights on several occasions here!

You can use other case studies that you may be aware of to build up the evidence.

Activity

Use the information above to elaborate upon the case that motives for corporate social responsibility matter. What else might each thinker/idea contribute? What might be possible difficulties with their views?

The case for the defence

The results are good so the motives of the defendant do not matter

Evidence for motives not mattering might include the following thinkers/ideas:

Adam Smith: People who worry about motives do not really understand how capitalism works. Looking after all the stakeholders creates happy customers who spend more money. It makes sense to be ethical purely for this reason.

Milton Friedman: The business has no responsibility to be ethical. At the moment profit is being made from the ethical branding. The owner should not worry about being unethical if in a few years that turns out to be a better way of making money.

Utilitarianism: It's all about outcome and results. Behaving in an ethical way generally makes more money and creates more happiness. The motive behind the action doesn't matter if the results are the same.

I'll see you in court

You can work through the process below individually either verbally or in written form (sometimes verbalising thoughts is the first step to being able to write them down), or you could work through the activities as a group or class, debating and reaching a verdict.

The judge opens the case: What is corporate social responsibility? Is it about the actions or the motive? What are some of the key issues in business ethics?

The case for the prosecution is presented: The motive of CSR does matter. What are the key arguments in favour of this position? What key evidence would be presented?

Defence cross-examination: What are the issues arising from this evidence? What counterarguments can be brought forward?

The case for the defence is presented: The motive of CSR doesn't matter. What are the key arguments in favour of this position? What key evidence would be presented?

Prosecution cross-examination: What are the issues arising from this evidence? What counterarguments can be brought forward?

Closing speeches: What is the key piece of evidence for the prosecution case? What is the key piece of evidence for the defence case?

Jury decision: What conclusion do you reach? Why? (If you are doing this exercise as a class/group you can take a vote.)

Activities

Core

1. Create a large concept map that outlines the case for a genuine interest in corporate social responsibility.
2. Create a large concept map that outlines the case against a genuine interest in corporate social responsibility.
3. Write a speech to use in the court case – select one of the arguments or scholars. Make your speech persuasive by adding justified reasons and examples to support your view.

Stretch

4. Write questions to ask the defence and prosecution witnesses. Make them as tricky as possible.

5. Think about possible answers to your questions – how could you respond and challenge the witness further? (This is developing the skill of critical analysis found in AO2 Level 6.)

Challenge

6. 'The trouble with corporate social responsibility is that it is not genuine; people are just pretending to tick ethical boxes so as to increase their profits.' Is this a fair point?
   Using the material in this chapter, write a detailed response to this claim using examples.

Wrap up

1 What is the name given to the idea that a business has wider ethical responsibilities to all its stakeholders?

2 What does Milton Friedman believe about corporate social responsibility?

3 What would a Kantian believe about whistleblowing?

4 What would a utilitarian believe about whistleblowing?

5 What is the name given to the belief that it is important to acquire material things?

6 Why might globalisation have been a good thing for places such as India and China?

7 Which ethical theory may express the concern that people in developing countries are treated as a means to an end as businesses pursue lower production costs?

8 What might a utilitarian think about whether good ethics is good business?

9 'The theory is particularly time-consuming and requires numerous variables be considered' – is this a key weakness of a utilitarian or a Kantian approach to business?

10 'It is also difficult to know what to do if there are conflicting duties to the various stakeholders' – is this a key weakness of a utilitarian or a Kantian approach to business?

GET READY

Summarising

1 Create a set of flash cards for the technical terms that you have come across during the lessons and your independent study. Test yourself on the definitions.

Linking

2 Draw together: Produce a concept map or use an online concept-mapping tool such as Coggle to review the topic and show the links between the key ideas.

Debate

3 'Business is business – there is no need to complicate the issue by worrying about ethics.'

Discuss this in small groups and make a note of the points raised. Add them to your notes. You could hold a class debate and vote on the issue.

Going further

4   Which of the ethical theories you have studied do you think provides the better approach to business ethics? Give reasons for your answer.

5   The material you have created in Questions 1 and 2 above could be turned into an essay plan. Practise your essay skills by turning one of the reasons into a paragraph.

CHECKLIST

I know, understand and can ...

- ☐ explain the idea of corporate social responsibility

- ☐ explain with examples the idea of whistleblowing

- ☐ explain the idea that good ethics is also good business

- ☐ explain what is meant by globalisation and how this is linked to this topic

- ☐ explain and assess how well the theory of utilitarianism addresses the issues in business ethics

- ☐ explain and assess how well the theory of Kantian ethics addresses the issues in business ethics

- ☐ assess whether corporate social responsibility is genuine or whether businesses are merely going through the ethical motions

- ☐ assess whether globalisation encourages or discourages business being ethical

- ☐ consider whether humans can flourish in our capitalist consumerist society.

Get practising

Ask the expert

'I do A level Business Studies and Geography as my other two subjects. Can I use things that I have learned in these subjects to answer questions in RS?' – *Ashleigh*

The expert says: Absolutely. Any material that is relevant and helps to answer the question will be credited. As with everything else in essay writing, you will need to carefully explain any examples or ideas that you bring in so that it is clear what is being said.

'Could you settle an argument between myself and Liam? When we apply utilitarianism or Kant to business ethics, I think this is AO1 but Liam says it is AO2. Which of us is right?' – *Sophie*

The expert says: You are correct that applying an ethical theory to an issue is AO1 – you are showing knowledge and understanding of how the theory can be used. AO2 comes when the theory is assessed and you are trying to say how good the theory is in terms of addressing the issue.

In addition to your work in other subjects, this topic is very much a live and current topic. It is likely that news stories will break that directly relate to some of the issues in this topic. Be prepared to add examples to your notes and don't be afraid to use them in the exam.

Exam skills: Depth of AO1

To get high grades, you need to show depth in terms of your explanation of ideas. This requires a selection of relevant material, in-depth understanding, good use of technical terms and a range of views. This is not necessarily writing more words – quality is better than quantity. As you practise AO1 skills it may be worth giving yourself a word limit, for example 100 words, with the aim of packing as much detail into those words as possible.

In the examples below, the students are attempting to explain how Kantian ethics may apply to business.

Izzy's answer

Kantian ethics involves hypothetical and categorical imperatives. Kant believed that all human beings have duties and that people should carry out their duties. In business the main duty is to make money, as this is what is important to the company. So there would be no requirement to care for other people, such as suppliers in the developing world. Kant also believes in treating people as ends and this would mean that you would have to put people's rights above whether or not money is being made.

There is some understanding here but it is not clear or at a high level. If you imagine an educated person who has not studied RS trying to make sense of this, they would be left with many questions. The first sentence is not developed and it is not clear that the student knows how hypothetical and categorical imperatives link to the rest of the theory. The point on duty to make money seems to be a misunderstanding given the sentence after it. It might be possible to apply Kant in this way but the student has not unpacked this. The final part is a little better, but 'people as ends' needs a little explanation; an example might help to show that the point is understood.

Jack's answer

Kantian ethics rests on Kant's idea that morality is *a priori* synthetic; moral truths can be logically deduced by reason. Kant argues that we must follow our duty, which can be worked out by identifying the categorical imperative (a command that we should obey) rather than the hypothetical imperative (a command that we are not obliged to follow but would only do so if we wanted the outcome). One of the formulations of the categorical imperative is the requirement that we treat human beings as an end not as a means to an end. This is very relevant to business ethics as businesses in the developed world repeatedly exploit workers in the developing world; workers are essentially slaves in sweat shops earning little but producing cheap clothes for Europe and America. Kant would argue that such conditions are morally wrong as they treat the individuals involved badly, robbing them of their dignity.

In this answer key terms are introduced with a little explanation that establishes that Jack has a detailed understanding of Kantian ethics. The example also helps show that Jack is not just remembering what he has revised but genuinely understands the content.

Activity

Write a similar paragraph on utilitarianism on business. Try to pack as much as possible into around 100 words.

CHAPTER 7

Meta-ethical theories

Big picture

Unlike the other topics in Religion and Ethics, which look at questions within ethics, the topic of meta-ethics looks at the subject of ethics as a whole. It asks what we mean when we use ethical terms such as 'good', 'right' and 'evil'. Do these words describe real things that actually exist or are they just our feelings about certain actions?

Engage

Consider the situations below.

1 Imagine that you are asked to describe an ice cream. You might suggest that it is cold, creamy, is a solid, has a certain shape, tastes like vanilla. Suppose your friend points out that you have missed something in your description. You have left out the 'niceness' or 'tastiness' of the ice cream. Is 'niceness' something that is factually true of the ice cream or is it just a matter of opinion? In a sense, the topic of meta-ethics is engaging in a similar debate over moral ideas such as 'goodness'.

2 Look at the first mini-conversation below (number 1). Which of the other two conversations (numbers 2 and 3) is most similar to it? Why do you think that is?

▲ If we were to say that the ice cream was nice, what would we mean?

1 'Eating animals is wrong.'   'There is nothing wrong in sometimes eating meat.'

2 'Paris is the capital of France'   'No, Berlin is the capital of France.'

3 'That film was fantastic.'   'I disagree, it was dreadful.'

3 Apart from ethical discussions, are there other subject areas where it is unclear whether something is factual or merely a matter of opinion?

The specification

Content	Key knowledge
Key ideas of meta-ethics, including: ● naturalism ● intuitionism ● emotivism	● What it is (the belief that values can be defined in terms of some natural property in the world) and its application to absolutism ● What it is (the belief that basic moral truths are indefinable but self-evident) and its application to the term 'good' ● What it is (the belief that ethical terms evince (indicate) approval or disapproval) and its application to relativism

Learners should have the opportunity to discuss issues related to meta-ethics, including:
● whether or not what is meant by the word 'good' is the defining question in the study of ethics
● whether or not ethical terms such as 'good', 'bad', 'right' and 'wrong':
  • have an objective factual basis that makes them true or false in describing something
  • reflect only what is in the mind of the person using such terms
  • can be said to be meaningful or meaningless
● whether or not, from a common-sense approach, people just know within themselves what is good, bad, right and wrong.

7.1 What are the key questions and theories of meta-ethics?

Aim

Gain an overview of the key ideas in this topic.

Starter

What is the topic of meta-ethics about? Without looking at the previous page, try to write an answer in one or two sentences.

The 'levels' of ethical discussion

There are different levels of discussion when it comes to ethics. This is a little bit like the levels of questions we might get in another subject, such as music or football. We can ask very specific questions, such as whether abortion is right or whether lying is wrong in a particular situation. These practical issues are known as applied ethics. We can also ask more general questions about how we decide what is right or wrong, or which of the ethical theories will typically provide us with the best answers to moral dilemmas. This search for rules (or norms) is called normative ethics. Meta-ethics asks an even bigger question – it questions whether right and wrong even exist and asks what it is that we are doing when we speak of right and wrong.

Level of ethical discussion	Comparison with discussion of music
Applied, for example: ● Was it right for her to steal the bread? ● Is war ever justified?	Discussion of individual songs, for example: ● Does repeating the chorus work? ● Should the bass be louder?
Normative, for example: ● What is the best approach to ethical issues? ● Is it about happiness (utilitarianism) or duty (Kant)?	Discussion of general principles, for example: ● How good is Ed Sheeran's music? ● Is rock better than rap?
Meta-ethics, for example: ● Is there such a thing as right and wrong? ● What do these words mean?	Discussion of music from an outside perspective, for example: ● What purpose does music have? ● Is 'good music' a matter of opinion?

Two connected debates

One way of thinking about meta-ethics is to understand the topic as two connected debates. First, meta-ethics is a discussion about the *meaning* of ethical words such as 'good', 'bad', 'right' and 'wrong'. Are they statements that can in some sense be true or false, or do these words have some other function? If we state that 'He is wearing a green hat' or 'Liverpool is further north than London' it is clear that these sentences will be either true or false. Other things we say are not making claims about the world, however. When we shout 'Hurray!' or utter a swear word, it would be strange if someone asked us whether our cheer or curse was true or not!

Key terms

Cognitive – The belief that moral statements are able to be true or false
Non-cognitive – The belief that moral statements are not subject to truth or falsity

Tip

You will also use the terms cognitive and non-cognitive in Chapter 9 of the Philosophy of Religion unit, Twentieth-century perspectives.

● Some philosophers see moral language as **cognitive** – when we say 'Murder is wrong', we are saying something that can be shown to be either true or false, in the same way that 'It is raining outside' can be true or false.

● Other philosophers disagree and suggest that moral language is **non-cognitive** – when we make a moral statement, we are merely expressing our feelings on an issue. It is not in any sense true or false.

The second, related debate in meta-ethics is about *reality and existence*. Some philosophers are realists and argue that moral truths actually exist and are real features of the world. Other philosophers, known as anti-realists, reject this, claiming that there are no moral truths in the world.

These two debates – the one about meaning and the one about existence – are connected in this topic.

Three main theories

The specification (see page 93) looks at three main meta-ethical theories.

1 **Naturalism:** Suggests that 'good', 'bad', 'right' and 'wrong' can be observed and discovered empirically – using our senses – in the same way that we find out other facts about the world around us. Naturalism is a realist and cognitive theory.

2 **Intuitionism:** Suggests that 'good', 'bad', 'right' and 'wrong' actually exist but cannot be seen or discovered in the same way as other facts. Moral truths are self-evident and are known by intuition. Intuitionism is a realist and cognitive theory.

3 **Emotivism:** Rejects the view that 'good', 'bad', 'right' and 'wrong' actually exist. When we make moral statements, we are simply showing our opinions and feelings. Emotivism is an anti-realist and non-cognitive theory.

Naturalism

Intuitionism

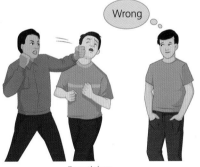

Emotivism

▲ Where is the 'wrongness'?

Activities

Core

1 What does the word 'cognitive' mean? List two cognitive theories of meta-ethics.

2 What does the word 'non-cognitive' mean? Which of the theories is non-cognitive?

3 Look at the cartoons on the left. Match up each quote below with the correct theory shown in the cartoons:

a 'I feel that it is wrong to hit others. The "wrongness" is my subjective reaction to what I am observing.'

b 'I can see the impact and hear the cry of pain. I am able to empirically observe that this act of hitting someone is wrong.'

c 'I know what has occurred is wrong. Although I can't see or hear wrongness, it is obvious to me that hitting this person is wrong.'

Stretch

4 Explain the differences between normative ethics and meta-ethics. Which area do you consider to be most important? Give a reason for your answer.

5 What is the main difference between naturalism and intuitionism?

Challenge

6 Making links: The ideas of cognitive and non-cognitive approaches to language are also used in the Philosophy of Religion module, in the Religious language and twentieth-century perspectives topics. If you have already studied this topic, draw a diagram similar to the ones on the left explaining different attitudes to language used about God.

7.2 Can moral values be understood as describing a natural property of the world?

Learn about the ideas of naturalism: that 'good', 'bad', 'right' and 'wrong' are natural properties of the world.

Starter

In his book *The Philosophy Gym*, philosopher Stephen Law gives the example of alien visitors Flib and Flob witnessing a mugging. Their earthling companion explains that what they have seen is wrong. The aliens are puzzled and explain that they have similar senses and have seen the purse being taken, the robber running away, heard the shouts, etc., but they cannot with any of their senses detect this idea of 'wrongness'. How could you explain to them?

Key terms

Naturalism The belief that moral values can be defined in terms of some natural property of the world
Naturalistic Fallacy The error of reducing goodness to a property that is found in nature, for example, pleasure

Where is the wrongness?

▲ Could you help aliens like Flib and Flob recognise 'wrongness'?

What is naturalism?

Naturalism is a type of moral realism. It agrees with intuitionism (see page 98) that facts exist about what is right and wrong. It is a cognitivist theory claiming that when we make moral claims, the statements we make are able to be either true or false. The distinctive point that naturalism makes is that these moral truths are able to be discovered by observation of the world around us. They are thus empirical facts.

There are a number of different views within naturalism, but they all have in common this idea that moral values can be empirically discovered.

Types of naturalism

One version of naturalism can be found in applying the natural law ideas of Aquinas that you may have looked at in Chapter 1. Aquinas views the world as having a God-given natural order that we can discover through observation and reasoning. Everything in the world, including ourselves, has a purpose (*telos*) and we can observe how good something is by asking whether it is fulfilling its purpose.

The philosopher John Stuart Mill (1806–73) offers a different type of naturalism that is based on his utilitarianism. As we observe the world, we are able to see that certain actions lead to pleasure and certain actions lead to pain; this enables us to discover what is right and wrong. He argues that the fact that human beings desire certain pleasures and goods must mean that it is a fact that these things are desirable – good in themselves.

Generally, naturalism is thought to lead to a moral absolutism as fixed truths about the world are being discovered. It is certainly true that people who adopt the naturalist position do tend towards absolutism in terms of normative ethics. However, it is entirely possible to be a naturalist on utilitarian grounds and thus to discover more relative truths in the world.

Analyse and evaluate

Naturalism is right to say that moral values are a feature of the world because:	Naturalism is wrong to say that moral values are a feature of the world because:
Mill argues that we are able to know what is good or desirable as these are the things that people actually desire. The very fact that people all want happiness is enough to show that happiness is actually a good thing.	Hume rejects the conventional wisdom of his day that right and wrong can be observed. There is a fact–value distinction or gap. He is concerned that we move too easily from factual statements ('is' and 'is not') to moral statements ('ought' and 'ought not'). Similar to the example of Flib and Flob in the Starter activity, he adds that when we consider an action that is wrong, we cannot empirically detect the vice or wrongness (see quote on page 99).
Naturalists might also point to the fact that there is significant agreement on moral values throughout the world. The fact that we largely agree on what is right and wrong suggests this is a factual matter (similar to us agreeing that bricks are a solid and not a liquid or gas) rather than a matter of opinion (such as discussion of whether an artist's music is good).	Naturalism is also guilty of a thinking error called the **naturalistic fallacy**. This claims that if something is natural, then it must be good. We may be wrong to equate the two, however. Nature has given us sharp teeth that makes it natural for us to eat meat – it may even bring us pleasure to do so, yet we cannot jump from this to the conclusion that it would be morally wrong to be a vegetarian.
Naturalists also worry that reducing morality to a matter of taste or opinion reduces the significance of ethical debates. Discussing whether or not killing is wrong is not the same as discussing food preferences.	G.E. Moore offers a criticism of Mill's naturalism in his open question argument (see page 98). Pleasure cannot be the same thing as goodness as it is still possible to ask if the pleasure is truly good. For example, eating chips is a pleasure, but we can still ask whether this is truly good.
	Some forms of naturalism, particularly that of Aquinas, make the assumption that there is a purpose or *telos* for humans, and this may ultimately require the existence of God. Many modern philosophers, including Sartre with his existentialism, would reject these assumptions. If there is no definite purpose, there cannot be any definite ideas on goodness.

Activities

Core

1 How does naturalism differ from intuitionism?
2 How does Aquinas' view differ from Mill's?
3 Why is it argued that there is a link between naturalism and absolutism?

Stretch

4 One of the arguments for naturalism claims that there is widespread agreement on moral truths. Write a paragraph explaining this and considering whether this is actually true. Use examples to illustrate your answer.
5 Explain what is meant by the naturalistic fallacy.

Challenge

6 Hume's point is that it is difficult to bridge the gap between the facts of a matter and the moral value. Research John Searle's answer to fact–value distinction. Does his response work?

7.3 Do people just know what is right and wrong?

Aim

Investigate the idea of intuitionism that moral values are indefinable and self-evident.

Starter

Make a list of objects that are typically yellow. Without referring to these objects, write a definition of what 'yellow' is that would be helpful to someone who has never seen the colour. How difficult is this?

Key term

Intuitionism The belief that moral values can be defined in terms of some natural property of the world

Recognising the problem

Intuitionism is mainly associated with the philosopher G.E. Moore (1873–1958). Moore accepts Hume's point that there seems to be a gap between facts and values (the 'is' and the 'ought'), hence naturalism is wrong to suggest that moral values can be discovered.

In his book *Principia Ethica*, Moore explores this problem with his open question argument. He suggests that there are two types of questions that we can ask:

- Closed questions are questions where only one answer is actually possible. For example, if we are told that someone is a bachelor, the question 'Is he unmarried?' only has one possible answer (it is like asking if a particular triangle happens to have three sides).

- Open questions are questions where several different answers are possible. For example, asking if a bachelor's hair is brown could have several possible answers. Likewise, the question 'Does the triangle have a right angle?' has more than one possible answer.

Moore uses this to reject naturalism. If Mill is right that pleasure is good, then it ought to be a closed question to ask if something that brings pleasure is really good. This is not the case, however. Something that brings us pleasure may or may not be good; it is an open question. This problem arises whenever we try to define what is good in terms of something that is observable in the world.

Understanding 'good'

Although Moore thinks that 'goodness' cannot be defined, he is a cognitivist and realist. There are truths about what is right and wrong. Goodness is known intuitively; it is indefinable but self-evident. To explain what this means, Moore makes a comparison with the colour 'yellow'. We would struggle if we were asked to define what yellowness is, yet each of us knows and recognises the colour and is able to point to it. Similarly, goodness cannot be described but we can point to many examples that we 'just know' are good.

Moore argues that 'good' is a simple idea. Like the concept of yellow, it cannot be broken into parts or properties. A complex idea might be something like a horse, where we could list the parts or break the idea down into components, for example legs, mane, ears, etc. We cannot list the parts of yellowness or goodness because they are simple ideas.

◄ We can list the properties or parts of a horse, but can you do the same for 'yellow'?

> ## Key quote
>
> 'If I am asked "What is good?" my answer is that good is good, and that is the end of the matter. Or if I am asked "How is good to be defined?" my answer is that it cannot be defined, and that is all I have to say about it.'
> (G.E. Moore, *Principia Ethica*)

Analyse and evaluate

Intuitionism is right to say that moral values are indefinable and self-evident because:	Intuitionism is wrong to say that moral values are indefinable and self-evident because:
Unlike naturalism, intuitionism takes the fact–value problem seriously and does not attempt to find moral values through observation of the world.	Although there is much moral agreement in the world, there is a significant amount of disagreement on many issues. This is a particular difficulty for intuitionists, who would claim that these truths are self-evident to all. One intuitionist, Pritchard, has attempted to address this by arguing that the intuitions of some people are better than those of others.
Intuitionism recognises that there is considerable moral agreement in the world.	Intuitionism seems unscientific and a little far-fetched. It is not clear what this strange 'faculty or power of intuition' actually is. It is certainly not something that can be scientifically analysed. Thus evolutionary explanations of morality such as those offered by Dawkins or psychological explanations such as those given by Freud (see Chapter 8) may be better accounts of morality.
Unlike emotivism, intuitionism is able to establish moral facts and ensure that 'right' and 'wrong' are not just a matter of taste or opinion.	If moral values are not empirical and we 'just know' what is right and wrong, there seems little difference between this and our 'just feeling' certain things are right or wrong. This would lead us towards emotivism.
	Intuitionism makes ethics seem like maths, where truths are self-evident and just obviously true. They are not the same, however. Mathematicians do not argue about what 5x7 might equate to and, unlike in ethics, if there were such an argument in maths it could be resolved using concrete examples.

Activities

Core

1   Write an example of a closed question and an open question.
2   What does G.E. Moore think is the key issue that naturalism fails to address?
3   According to Moore, why is goodness a simple idea rather than a complex idea?

Stretch

4   It is claimed that the moral agreement in the world supports intuitionism and thus moral disagreement would oppose intuitionism. Write a paragraph considering this point and reaching a conclusion.
5   Examine the weaknesses of intuitionism. Which do you consider to be the biggest weakness? Write a paragraph explaining the point and why it is so strong.

Challenge

6   Research Hume's view of how we acquire abstract ideas (the Internet Encyclopedia of Philosophy may be a good place to start). If Hume is right, how would this counteract intuitionism?

7.4 Do the ideas of right and wrong merely show approval and disapproval of actions?

Aim

Learn about emotivism: that 'right' and 'wrong' are terms that merely show approval or disapproval of actions.

Starter

In the ice cream example (page 93) we saw that emotivism was a **non-cognitivist** and **anti-realist** view of meta-ethics. It suggests that moral values are **subjective**. In pairs, check that each of you understands the words in bold.

Key term

Emotivism The belief that ethical terms evince (show) approval or disapproval

Tip

If you have already studied the verification principle in the Philosophy of Religion unit, you may want to review your notes as emotivism uses this principle.

Key quote

'Take any action allowed to be vicious ... examine it in all its lights and see if you can find that matter of fact ... which you call vice. You will never find it, till you turn your reflection into your own breast, and find a sentiment of disapprobation [disapproval] which arises in you, toward the action ... tis the object of feeling, not reason.'
(David Hume, *A Treatise of Human Nature*)

The fork and the Circle

Emotivism as a meta-ethical theory comes from A.J. Ayer (1910–89). Ayer's verification principle, which provides the background to his ideas, owes a great deal to the ideas of David Hume as well as a group of early twentieth-century Austrian philosophers known as the Vienna Circle.

Hume argues that there are two types of knowledge that philosophers can obtain:

- **Relation of ideas:** *A priori* knowledge of how ideas relate to each other, e.g. that 2 added to 3 makes 5.
- **Matters of fact:** *A posteriori* knowledge of things we can observe in the world, e.g. that water boils at 100 degrees.

These are the two prongs of Hume's fork. Hume famously argues that any books that do not contain either of the above should be 'committed to the flames'.

The Vienna Circle was influenced by Wittgenstein's early philosophy and shared his view that the aim of philosophy was the analysis of language to determine what was 'sense' and what was 'nonsense'. They suggested that statements were only meaningful if they could be verified (shown to be true) by the senses.

Ayer's verification principle

Ayer's verification principle combines the above ideas. He argues that a statement is meaningful if it is either:

- **An analytic statement:** It is true by definition, for example 'The bachelor is unmarried'.

Or:

- **A synthetic statement:** It is possible to say how (at least in theory) it would be possible to verify it, for example 'The cat is asleep at 4 a.m.'

Any statements that do not fit into these categories are not cognitive and are thus meaningless. Moral statements are not obviously logical nor can any matter of fact prove them to be true. So ethical statements are factually meaningless.

How to understand ethical statements

Ayer is concerned not with what ethical statements mean, but with what they are for. What are people doing when they use the words 'good', 'bad', 'right' and 'wrong'? He argues that ethical statements are simply expressions of personal preferences or emotions. Again, Ayer is influenced by Hume, who was one of the first philosophers to link morality to feelings rather than reason (see key quote on the left from Hume).

If I say that you were wrong to tell a lie, the word 'wrong' doesn't add any factual content. I might as well say 'You told a lie' in a disapproving tone. The key quote sums up Ayer's view succinctly.

Key quote

'The presence of an ethical symbol in a proposition adds nothing to its factual content. Thus if I say to someone, "You acted wrongly in stealing that money," I am not saying anything more than if I had simply said, "You stole that money." In adding that this action is wrong I am not making any further statement about it. I am simply evincing my moral disapproval of it. It is as if I had said, "You stole that money," in a peculiar tone of horror, or written it with the addition of some special exclamation marks.'

(A.J. Ayer, *Language, Truth, and Logic*)

Tip

One common issue with explanations of emotivism is that students suggest emotivists base decisions about what is right and wrong on their emotions, for example that euthanasia is wrong because we have negative feelings towards it. This shows a fundamental misunderstanding of the topic of meta-ethics. The position of the emotivist is not that right and wrong are discovered by the emotions, but rather that there is no such thing as right and wrong and that statements where we use these words are merely expressing or 'evincing' emotions.

Analyse and evaluate

Emotivism is right to suggest that moral statements merely show approval and disapproval of actions because:	Emotivism is wrong to suggest that moral statements merely show approval and disapproval of actions because:
Emotivism has an easier task in explaining why people have different moral views on many topics. There are no 'facts' about right and wrong, there are just feelings and attitudes.	Emotivism renders debate and discussion of ethics useless. In philosophical debate, one seeks to persuade the other to change their position by providing reasons, yet this would seem futile if both sides are merely expressing feelings and attitudes. Critics have suggested that debate then becomes a 'boo-hurray' shouting match.
Emotivism avoids the issue of the naturalistic fallacy, which causes great difficulty for the naturalist, as it rejects the idea that moral values are linked to anything in the world; they are merely the product of our sentiments.	Emotivism can also be said to trivialise ethical discussion. The philosopher Philippa Foot cites the example of concentration camps to suggest that Ayer's view cannot be right. There are significant ethical debates that should not be reduced to a matter of opinion.
Emotivism recognises that disputes in ethics are often driven by feelings rather than reasons. This echoes the work of psychologist Daniel Goleman on emotional intelligence, in which he argues that the emotional part of our brain reacts before the reasoning part kicks in.	Even for some non-cognitivists, the idea that we are merely expressing feelings and attitudes is not a complete description of what moral language is aiming to do. R.M. Hare has argued that moral language is in fact prescriptive; it is an attempt to persuade others to adopt our view.

Activities

Core

1 Give your own example of an analytic statement and a synthetic statement.
2 Why does Ayer think that ethical language is meaningless?
3 According to Ayer, what function does ethical language have?

Stretch

4 Explain how Hume and the Vienna Circle influence Ayer's thinking.

5 Does emotivism provide a good account of moral language? Give reasons for your answer.

Challenge

6 An alternative non-cognitive account of ethics is found in R.M. Hare's prescriptivism. Research this theory. How does it compare to emotivism?

7.5 The Big Debate: Are ethical terms meaningful or meaningless?

Aim

Consider the arguments for and against cognitive and non-cognitive views of meta-ethics.

Starter

Copy and complete the table at the top of the page to check your understanding of each of the three main meta-ethical theories.

Theory	Realist	Anti-realist	Cognitive	Non-cognitive
Naturalism				
Intuitionism				
Emotivism				

Considering the debate between the two sides

Some meta-ethical theories are realist and cognitive and thus view ethical language as meaningful. Other theories are anti-realist and non-cognitive and thus view ethical language as meaningless. A preliminary step in deciding which theory is right is to first consider the debate between these two sides.

Analyse and evaluate

Ethical terms can be argued to be meaningful because:	Ethical terms can be argued to be meaningless because:
There is widespread agreement over what is good and what is evil or wrong. These standards are broadly similar across cultures, for example the golden rule of not doing to others what you would not want done to you. This would not be the case if morality was merely a matter of opinion, for example there is no consensus on what is a good piece of music or a good film, but there is agreement in science where facts can be proved.	In *Ethics: Inventing right and wrong*, John Mackie gives three arguments:
But see the point opposite on moral relativism – perhaps it depends on whether you see the glass as half-full or half-empty! Likewise, agreement may not demonstrate moral facts but may demonstrate that human societies when faced with similar issues have responded with similar feelings and attitudes.	1 Relativism: Mackie argues that there is too much disagreement about what is right and wrong for ethical judgements to be a factual matter.
If ethical terms describe something real and factual then we can speak intelligently about ideas of moral progress. For example, we might suggest that human beings have better moral standards now that slavery has been abolished and same-sex marriage has been legalised. Yet the words 'better' or 'worse' presuppose that there is an actual standard that we are progressing towards or away from. If there were no such thing as right and wrong, it would make no sense to speak of progress, as the removal of slavery would be just a change, there would be no good to progress towards.	

If there were no such thing as right or wrong then this would require that we tolerate different answers to issues of right and wrong. While we may be able to do so for some topics – we may agree to differ on sexual matters or on euthanasia – it is not clear that tolerance can be given across all topics. Some philosophers have argued that tolerance becomes a paradox: not only are we required to tolerate the intolerable, but in insisting upon tolerance we actually end up enforcing tolerance as a moral truth – thus defeating our initial argument!	2 Empiricism: Mackie supports Hume in arguing that there is nothing available to our senses that would give us the ideas of right and wrong. It is thus more logical to assume that these ideas are purely human inventions. However, while this may be an effective objection to naturalism, it does not apply to intuitionism as the moral truths we discover here are not empirically observed.
One logical consequence of a lack of values and the lack of meaning in ethical statements is that nothing ultimately matters (nihilism). For thinkers such as Nietzsche, this should be seen as an opportunity as we are able to create our own values to replace those that we do not like. Yet this may also lead to alarming consequences: if I were to decide that playing the guitar loudly was the true good in life and that rules about murder were values that I now rejected in order to pursue this aim, then there is no reason why I ought not kill my neighbours when they complain about my limited but loud musicianship.	3 'Queerness': Mackie's third argument stems from the fact that if 'good', 'bad', 'right' and 'wrong' were to actually exist, they would be very unusual things. Mackie's word for this is that they are 'queer' – in its older meaning of being odd or unusual. Moral ideas are action-guiding; we behave differently as a result of having them. The reason I do not take your bag is because I have a belief about stealing. Ordinary empirical facts do not tend to guide our actions in quite the same way, which would lead to the conclusion that, whatever right and wrong are, they are not facts.
	Unverifiable: Linked to Mackie's point on empiricism is the idea that right and wrong are meaningless as they are unverifiable. They are not tautologies (statements that are true by definition) nor can we say how we might possibly confirm using our senses that stealing is wrong. This again would not necessarily rule out intuitionism, however, and critics of Ayer's verification principle have pointed out that it fails its own test.

Activities

Core

1 How does the verification principle make moral claims meaningless?

2 How does the argument about moral progress support the idea that moral language is meaningful?

3 What is nihilism and why is it relevant to this discussion?

Stretch

4 Consider the arguments on moral agreement and relativism. Which one do you agree with most? Write a paragraph explaining your reasons.

5 Explain Mackie's argument from queerness in your own words. Do you think he is right?

Challenge

6 Have a go at reading Chapter 1 of John Mackie's *Ethics: Inventing right and wrong*. It is quite hard in places, but you should be able to get the gist of what he is saying.

7.6 Is discussion about the meaning of ethical terms the most important debate in ethics?

Aim

Assess whether the debates raised in this topic are the most important ethical debates of all.

Starter

Without looking at your notes, write one or two sentences explaining what this topic, meta-ethics, is about. Attempt the same for normative ethics (a word we have used to describe the theories covered in Chapter 4).

Meta-ethics: Discussion about meaning of ethical terms and nature of ethics, e.g. whether 'good' actually exists, what such words mean

Normative ethics: Discussion of systems and theories of ethical decision-making, e.g. utilitarianism, natural law

Applied ethics: Discussion of practical issues in ethical decision-making, e.g. euthanasia

▲ The three levels of ethical discussion

The growing interest in language

While discussion of whether goodness can be found or whether it is merely a matter of opinion go some way back in philosophy, it was in the twentieth century that a focus on language began to dominate philosophical thought. This was in part due to the influence of Wittgenstein, whose *Tractatus Logico-Philosophicus* (1919) made the argument that it was misunderstanding of language that was responsible for many philosophical problems. He suggested that philosophers were like flies trapped in a jar; by paying careful attention to language and the meaning of words, it would be possible to release the flies from the jar! Hence many philosophers, including the Vienna Circle and A.J. Ayer, began to focus on exploring ethical language, convinced that the difficulties in ethics were largely due to misunderstandings of language.

Key quote

'Philosophical problems arise when language goes on holiday.'
(Ludwig Wittgenstein, *Philosophical Investigations*)

'One can imagine rarified groups of Anglo-American philosophers arguing the toss over the precise meaning of right and wrong while social chaos and moral havoc is wreaked around them.'
(Peter Vardy, *The Puzzle of Ethics*)

MacIntyre's criticism of meta-ethics

The philosopher Alasdair MacIntyre (1929–) in his 1981 book *After Virtue* offers a criticism of modern meta-ethical philosophy. He argues that our society has dismantled key moral ideas such as *telos* but is seeking to use the old moral language and terminology to discuss moral ideas. Given that many thinkers have embraced the ideas of the existentialists that there is no ultimate truth or purpose, discussion of moral ideas is doomed to fail and will lead us logically to emotivism or a nihilism inspired by Nietzsche. For MacIntyre, the focus on meta-ethics is a distraction and misses the real point of ethics. This view is shared by Peter Vardy, as seen in the key quote.

Analyse and evaluate

Discussion of the meaning of ethical terms (meta-ethics) is the most important debate in ethics because:	*Discussion of the meaning of ethical terms (meta-ethics) is not the most important debate in ethics because:*
Meta-ethical discussion is by its nature the highest level of ethical discussion. Hence it could be argued that it is important to address the question of whether objective goodness exists before proceeding to a normative or applied level.	While theoretically meta-ethics may be important, on a practical level it has little relevance for day-to-day moral decision-making. It is a niche subject that is mainly considered by professional philosophers in universities, but it does not significantly affect decisions in the real world.
The meaning of terms is actually important and if meaning is not addressed then it would seem that Wittgenstein may be right that there is a danger of talking at cross-purposes and creating philosophical problems due to misunderstanding.	Similarly, even if meta-ethical discussion is felt to be important and takes place, further theory and discussion is required at a normative level since the question 'What should I do?' remains. Thus leading meta-ethicists G.E. Moore and R.M. Hare both argue for utilitarianism, and W.D. Ross for a version of Kantian ethics, as their meta-ethical theories did not touch practical concerns.
If we wish to prevent a descent into nihilism then this can only be done by focusing on meta-ethical questions.	MacIntyre in *After Virtue* expresses the view that a focus on meta-ethics has actually proved harmful to moral development. It has led to the emotivist position that moral judgements are just opinion and that it does not matter what views we adopt (nihilism). Thus we should refocus on normative theories so that we can share a view of what goodness or virtue is.

Activities

Core

1 How does the work of Wittgenstein suggest that meta-ethics may be most important?
2 What does MacIntyre think is the key problem with meta-ethical discussion?
3 Is meta-ethics or normative ethics more important? Give a reason for your answer.

Stretch

4 Look at the case in favour of meta-ethics being the most important debate in ethics. Rank the arguments. Which is most significant? Give a reason for your answer.

5 Look at the case in favour of normative ethics being more important. Rank the arguments. Which is most significant? Give a reason for your answer.

Challenge

6 MacIntyre's own view is that we should return to the ideas of virtue ethics that derive from Aristotle's work. Find out more about the ideas of virtue ethics. You may see that there are some links to natural law.

7.7 The Big Debate: Do moral terms only reflect what is in the mind of the person using such terms?

Aim

Draw together everything you have discussed in this chapter and use it to form a case either for or against objective moral facts. When you have heard both sides of the case, you decide the outcome.

Starter

Without looking at your notes, explain or define the following terms: cognitivism; non-cognitivism; naturalism; intuitionism; emotivism; relativism; nihilism. At the end of the task, check your understanding by comparing what you have written against your notes or this textbook.

Preparing the case

Are there objective moral facts or do the terms 'good', 'bad', 'right' and 'wrong' merely reflect people's personal ideas and feelings about moral issues?

The case for the prosecution

Moral facts **do not** exist

Evidence that there are no moral facts and that moral statements just reflect what is in people's minds might include the following thinkers or ideas:

A.J. Ayer: Moral truths or facts don't exist. The verification principle shows them to be factually meaningless. When people make moral statements, they are merely showing us their feelings or ideas on the issue.

John Mackie: Moral ideas are opinions, not facts. There is too much variation in the ideas that different societies and people have. Also, if moral facts did exist, they would be very odd or 'queer' compared to other facts.

Nietzsche: There are no moral truths. This presents an opportunity for the strong to put forward their moral ideas and gradually replace traditional Christian morality, which is based on weak moral ideas.

The case for the defence

Moral facts **do** exist, they are not just in the mind

Evidence that moral facts do exist independently of human minds may include the following thinkers/ideas:

> **Thomas Aquinas:** Nature reveals that people and actions have *telos* or purpose. We cannot randomly change this purpose.

> **J.S. Mill:** Our desires show us what is good; we desire certain things because they are in fact desirable.

> **G.E. Moore:** Goodness is a reality. It may not be empirical but it is self-evident to our intuition.

I'll see you in court

You can work through the process below individually either verbally or in written form (sometimes verbalising thoughts is the first step to being able to write them down), or you could work through the activities as a group or class, debating and reaching a verdict.

The judge opens the case: What is the topic of meta-ethics about? How do the theories of naturalism, intuitionism and emotivism answer the key question of whether moral facts exist or are just in the mind?

↓

The case for the prosecution is presented: There is no such thing as moral facts. What are the key arguments in favour of the view that moral statements reflect only what is in the mind? What key evidence would be presented?

↓

Defence cross-examination: What are the issues arising from this evidence? What counterarguments can be brought forward?

↓

The case for the defence is presented: Moral facts actually exist. What are the key arguments for suggesting that moral statements reflect more than just what is in people's minds? What key evidence would be presented?

→

Prosecution cross-examination: What are the issues arising from this evidence? What counterarguments can be brought forward?

↓

Closing speeches: What is the key piece of evidence for the prosecution case?
What is the key piece of evidence for the defence case?

↓

Jury decision: What conclusion do you reach? Why? (If you are doing this exercise as a class/group you can take a vote.)

Activities

Core

1 Create a large concept map that outlines the case in favour of moral facts.

2 Create a large concept map that outlines the case against moral facts.

3 Write a speech to use in the court case – select one of the arguments or scholars. Make your speech persuasive by adding justified reasons and examples to support your view.

Stretch

4 Write questions to ask the defence and prosecution witnesses. Make them as tricky as possible.

5 Think about possible answers to your questions – how could you respond and challenge the witness further? (This is developing the skill of critical analysis found in AO2 Level 6.)

Challenge

6 Write a conclusion for this debate. Did you/your class decide that moral facts exist or that they are just ideas in people's minds? Which evidence did you find most persuasive and why? Are there any doubts left? If so, what are the doubts and why were they not answered in the case? Can you think of ways to answer those doubts now?

Wrap up

QUIZ

1 Which meta-ethical theory can be described as non-cognitive?

2 Which meta-ethical theories can be described as cognitive?

3 What is the naturalistic fallacy?

4 Which philosopher likened our ability to recognise moral truths to our ability to recognise colour?

5 Which meta-ethical theory believes that moral statements can be established empirically?

6 What is the name for the idea that statements are meaningless unless they can be proved by sensory observation?

7 What is the name for the philosophical theory that there is no meaning in anything?

8 What is the name for the branch of ethics that deals with ethical theories such as Kantian ethics and utilitarianism?

9 The argument that there are significant differences in moral codes within the world can be used to support which of the three meta-ethical theories?

10 Which meta-ethical theory suggests that moral truths are both indefinable and self-evident?

GET READY

Summarising

1 Copy out the below key words and match them to the correct definitions given below.

Cognitive	The belief that ethical terms evince (show) approval or disapproval
Non-cognitive	The belief that moral statements are subject to being either true or false
Naturalism	The belief that moral statements are indefinable but self-evident
Intuitionism	The belief that moral values can be defined in terms of some natural property of the world
Emotivism	The belief that moral statements are not subject to being true or false

Applying

2 Spaced revision: Produce a spider diagram for each of the three main meta-ethical theories. Give three or four points to explain each theory (AO1), and two strengths and two weaknesses (AO2). Cover the diagrams and see how much you can remember without looking. Take a break for a couple of hours, then repeat this process. (This mirrors the process of trying to recall information in an exam and is called retrieval practice.)

Going further

3 For the brave: Look at the specification on page 93 and try to write a possible exam question. Bulletpoint (or write!) a model answer and get your teacher to mark it.

 Tip

One of the initial dangers of the topic of meta-ethics is that it seems quite unusual and remote. We might learn the material – what each theory says and some strengths and weaknesses – but not really get involved in the topic. The best essays on meta-ethics show engagement with the issues rather than rote learning. It is worth going back to page 94 and asking yourself whether something like murder or theft is actually factually wrong or whether it is just a matter of opinion. This may help you begin to form views on this topic.

CHECKLIST

I know, understand and can …

- ☐ explain and assess ethical naturalism
- ☐ explain and assess intuitionism
- ☐ explain and assess emotivism
- ☐ consider whether the meta-ethical question 'What is good?' is the key question in ethics
- ☐ assess whether ethical terms ('good', 'bad', 'right', 'wrong') are objective facts
- ☐ assess whether ethical terms ('good', 'bad', 'right', 'wrong') are meaningful or meaningless.

Get practising

Ask the expert

'I have always struggled with introductions to essays and I find myself writing up to half a page. My teacher says my introductions don't really say anything. How do I write a good introduction?' – Penny

Penny's first attempt

Penny is writing an essay assessing emotivism.

In this essay I will be assessing emotivism. Emotivism is a meta-ethical theory associated with A.J. Ayer (1910–89). Ayer was educated at Eton and Oxford and met members of the Vienna Circle and used the verification principle. The theory of emotivism says that moral statements are expressions of emotion, they are not factual. In this essay I will be looking at various arguments for and against emotivism and deciding which is the strongest. There are other meta-ethical theories including naturalism and intuitionism that give a different answer to emotivism. These need to be assessed before deciding whether emotivism is a successful theory.

Penny's introduction has a number of issues. It starts with the claim that she is going to be answering the question. We would hope that people do answer the question; she doesn't need to say this. Equally, we don't really need biographical information about thinkers. We are assessing their ideas. The paragraph is, like many introductions, caught in two minds. It is trying to be an introduction while also having elements of the first main paragraph. Penny should consider the CBA method (see the Tip box) or just start the essay; exam essays do not have to have introductions. An example of this approach is found in Adam's essay.

Adam's introduction

Emotivism is a meta-ethical theory that suggests moral judgements are based on emotion and are not factual. The theory is associated with A.J. Ayer and is opposed by other thinkers such as G.E. Moore. This essay will show that emotivism does not successfully explain moral language.

 Tip

When you do an assignment at university, you will need to have an introduction. This is not necessary in examination essays, however. That said, a good introduction does help to show the examiner where you are heading. One way of writing a good concise introduction is the CBA method:

C **Context:** What the topic/question is about
B **Brains:** Who the key thinkers might be
A **Line of argument:** What position you will take

CHAPTER 8

Conscience

Both extinction rebellion and Nelson Mandela could appeal to conscience to justify their actions

Big picture

We can all relate to feelings of guilt over things we should not have done or to having a sense that we should act in a certain way in a situation. We use the word 'conscience' to describe these ideas and feelings. It is unclear what this conscience is, however: it may be something that is God-given and part of our nature or it could equally be something that is caused by our surroundings. This topic will introduce you to two classic views of conscience.

Engage

1   Appeals to conscience are sometimes made when people do things that are against the laws of their day. Find out more about Extinction Rebellion or Nelson Mandela.

2   Without thinking too deeply, try to write a definition of 'conscience', and then attempt to refine your view by discussing the three either/or statements below with a partner.

EITHER Conscience is given to us by God	→	OR We acquire conscience from parents and society
EITHER Conscience is innate	→	OR Conscience is acquired
EITHER Conscience should be obeyed	→	OR Conscience can be ignored

The specification

Content	Key knowledge
• Aquinas' theological approach to conscience	• Details of this approach, including: • ratio (reason placed in every person as a result of being created in the image of God) • synderesis (inner principle directing a person towards good and away from evil) • conscientia (a person's reason making moral judgements) • vincible ignorance (lack of knowledge for which a person is responsible) • invincible ignorance (lack of knowledge for which a person is not responsible)
• Freud's psychological approach to conscience	• Details of this approach, including: • psychosexual development (early childhood awareness of libido) • id (instinctive impulses that seek satisfaction in pleasure) • ego (mediates between the id and the demands of social interaction) • superego (contradicts the id, works on internalised ideals from parents and society, and tries to make the ego behave morally)

Learners should have the opportunity to discuss issues related to ideas about conscience, including:
* comparison between Aquinas and Freud:
  * on the concept of guilt
  * on the presence or absence of God within the workings of the conscience and superego
  * on the process of moral decision-making
* whether conscience is linked to, or separate from, reason and the unconscious mind
* whether conscience exists at all or is instead an umbrella term covering various factors involved in moral decision-making, such as culture, environment, genetic predisposition and education.

8.1 How helpful is Aquinas' view of the conscience?

◀ Henry VIII would have had a different understanding of the conscience to that of Aquinas

Aim

Understand Aquinas' theological view of the conscience and consider how helpful his explanation of the phenomenon is.

Starter

'The King has found his conscience burdened with his present marriage … and considers it would be offensive to God and man if he were to persist in it, and with great remorse of conscience has now for a long time felt he is living under the offence of the Almighty.' (Cardinal Wolsey (1473–1530), Henry VIII's adviser)

'For one bishop of your opinion I have a hundred saints of mine … I have the general councils for 1,000 years … and all the Kingdoms of Christendom.' (St Thomas More)

Henry VIII describes an inner feeling, whereas St Thomas More refers to the tradition of the Church. Which is closer to your understanding of conscience?

Key terms

Synderesis The inner principle directing a person towards good and away from evil
Conscientia A person's reason making moral judgements

Ratio

It has been common in Christian thought to describe conscience as something intuitive, some sort of inner feeling similar to Wolsey's description of Henry VIII. More's view is that conscience cannot be personal and is instead a rational reflection on the moral standards held and passed down through tradition. This view is very close to that of Aquinas.

Aquinas argues that all humans are created with 'ratio' – reason placed in each of us as a result of being created in the image of God. Ratio is roughly translated as reason but Aquinas means a little more than that. Human beings are unique in being able to deliberate over moral matters. We have a God-given ability to consider all the information and reach a judgement. It is this key aspect that makes Aquinas' view of the conscience a theological one; God may not be directly communicating with us as in other views of conscience (e.g. Newman's, see page 113), but he has provided us with a powerful tool for moral decision-making.

Synderesis and conscientia

For Aquinas, conscience is our mind making moral decisions. Aquinas draws on two words used to describe conscience in the Bible and makes a subtle distinction between them:

- **Synderesis** is described as our natural desire to do good and avoid evil. This is the key precept of his natural law thinking (see pages 2–3). We are aware that this is a moral rule and we have a desire to fulfil it. We can use reasoning to develop the habit of synderesis, being fully aware of the moral rules.

- **Conscientia** is the name Aquinas gives to the process of forming moral judgements; the process of applying our knowledge to the unique circumstances that are before us. Again, this is something that we must practise in order to do efficiently.

Two types of mistakes – vincible and invincible ignorance

Aquinas argues that once conscience has reasoned, we are bound to follow the decision made. It is possible, however, that conscience can be mistaken. Aquinas is relatively optimistic about human nature and believes that humans do not deliberately choose acts that they know are evil; rather they make mistakes and pursue apparent goods.

Key quote

'Properly speaking, conscience is not a power but an act ...
The word "conscience" comes from *"cum alio scientia"*, that is knowledge applied to an individual case.'
(Aquinas, *Summa Theologica* 1 Q79)

As such, all wrong actions stem from ignorance, which comes in two types:

- **Vincible ignorance** is a lack of knowledge for which a person is responsible. Aquinas gives the example of someone committing adultery. The person has applied their reasoning incorrectly, believing that on some level the affair is good. They should, however, have known the divine law 'Do not commit adultery'. They are responsible for this lack of knowledge.

- **Invincible ignorance** is a lack of knowledge for which a person is not responsible. To illustrate this, Aquinas gives a highly implausible example. If a man were to sleep with someone other than his wife but whom he mistakenly believes is his wife (and she believes that he is her husband), then this is not something that he should be held morally responsible for.

Analyse and evaluate

Aquinas provides a helpful view of the conscience because:	Aquinas does not provide a helpful view of the conscience because:
Aquinas' view of the conscience puts reason and rationality centre stage. This could be seen as an improvement upon other theological views, *but* ... (See weakness 1)	(From strength 1) ... Aquinas' rational view does not fit with how we experience the phenomenon of conscience. We are conscious of a more immediate and intuitive sense rather than a process of deliberation and reflection.
Aquinas' view of the conscience provides a good explanation of moral disagreement. If conscience were directly linked to God as Newman thinks, then it is hard to see why people would disagree over right and wrong. By stressing individual reasoning in conscience, Aquinas is able to explain these issues.	Research carried out on moral development by thinkers such as Piaget and Kohlberg shows that moral thinking develops over time. It could be argued that this is a challenge to Aquinas' idea that synderesis is innate, although Aquinas may respond that synderesis is only one aspect of conscience.
Aquinas is also able to explain why someone may change their moral views over time, which is something that a more direct view of the conscience may struggle with.	Similarly, some thinkers argue that Aquinas fails to take into account the social and environmental factors that seem to affect people's moral views.
	Aquinas reaches the uncomfortable conclusion that we should obey our conscience even if it is in error. This does not seem helpful.
	Aquinas is perhaps guilty of being overly optimistic about human nature. His view of apparent goods is naïve, suggesting that people do not deliberately choose evil acts. His view of our rational abilities is also optimistic; Augustine's view of original sin and the divided will would be more cautious about our abilities.

Activities

Core

1 What is the difference between Aquinas' ideas and other theological accounts of the conscience?

2 What does Aquinas mean by synderesis and conscientia?

3 Give your own examples to illustrate vincible and invincible ignorance.

Stretch

4 Using the table above as a starting point, what are the strengths and weaknesses of Aquinas' view of the conscience? Use examples to explain each of your points.

5 How effective is Aquinas' account of the conscience? Write a one paragraph response.

Challenge

6 A more direct theological view of conscience is found in the work of J.H. Newman (1801–90), who believed conscience was the voice of God. Find out more about his view so that you can contrast it with that of Aquinas.

8.2 How helpful is Freud's view of the conscience?

Aim

Investigate Freud's approach to the conscience and consider how useful his ideas are.

Starter

Without looking at the previous page, match these key words and definitions that relate to Aquinas' view of the conscience.

Ratio	Lack of knowledge for which the person is not responsible
Synderesis	God-given reason that each of us possesses
Conscientia	Lack of knowledge for which the person is responsible
Vincible ignorance	A person's reason making the actual moral judgement
Invincible ignorance	The inner principle that guides us to pursue good and avoid evil

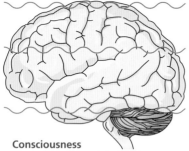

Consciousness
Those thoughts and desires that we can and do experience

Preconscious
Those thoughts and feelings that we aren't experiencing but may come to the surface at some point

Unconscious
The thoughts and feelings that are buried beneath the surface of our mind and cannot be retrieved, except by psychoanalysis

▲ The three layers of the mind

Key terms

Ego The part of our personality that mediates between the id and the demands of social interaction

Id The instinctive impulses that seek satisfaction in pleasure

Superego The internalised ideals from parents and society that tries to make the ego behave morally

Three layers of the mind

Sigmund Freud (1856–1939) believed that the mind was like a machine and the purpose of psychology was to uncover its workings. Conscience is just another one of these workings that psychology will be able to explain. Freud believed that the mind is made up of three layers (see diagram on the left).

Three aspects of personality

Human personality is formed in the unconscious and consists of three aspects:

● The **ego** is the conscious self. It is the part seen by the outside world and the thinking that we are most conscious of.

● The **id** is the unconscious self, which contains basic desires and drives – two key ones being sex and death. The id is our basic drives and passions.

● The **superego** is something that is within the ego – it is a reaction to the id. The superego is a set of moral controls and ideas given by authority and often opposed by the id. Freud is particularly interested in the superego (which he calls ego-ideal in his earlier books).

Effectively, by conscience Freud means the superego.

Forming the conscience

For Freud, conscience is superego and can be explained psychologically. It is formed by society, particularly by the parents. It is a reaction to all the demands that are placed upon a person that they cannot live up to. We start to internalise the voice of our parents, and this continues with every interaction with authority figures. A gap emerges between the ego (who we actually are) and the demands of the superego (our idea of an ideal person formed by all these early interactions).

Guilt occurs when we go against our conscience/superego. The superego 'retains the character of the father', but as we get older other masters and authority figures are also significant.

Psychosexual development

For Freud, all psychological problems are caused by sexuality. Freud observes that psychosexual development goes through several stages and the development may be either healthy or unhealthy (see table below). This is particularly seen in his theory of the Oedipus complex. In a male child's pre-sexual development, the child develops a fixation for his mother and views his father as an obstacle to the fulfilment of these sexual desires. The child both fears and is jealous of his father. These feelings, which are repressed, cause guilt and shame.

Stage	Age	Pleasure source	Explanation
Oral	0–1 years	Mouth	Pleasure is gained from sucking, biting and swallowing
Anal	1–3 years	Anus	Toilet training – pleasure gained from defecating or retaining faeces
Phallic	3–6 years	Genitals	Oedipus and Electra complexes – sexual dysfunction may develop

Analyse and evaluate

Freud's view is helpful because:	Freud's view is not helpful because:
Unlike Aquinas, Freud begins with our experience of guilt. This is how conscience initially reveals itself to us so it seems right to focus an explanation on this phenomenon.	(From strength 2) … Although in a sense Freud's work can be seen as empirical and scientific, the research that it is based on is limited. Freud's analysis was based on a small number of patients with psychological problems. It may be difficult to generalise from them to the whole population.
Freud's explanation is based on psychology rather than theology. In engaging in empirical research, he is attempting to be more scientific than some theological views of the conscience, *but* … (See weaknesses 1 and 2)	(From strength 2) … Furthermore, Karl Popper has accused Freud of being pseudo-scientific (not really scientific at all). He notes that scientific claims have the ability to be proved wrong if they are false. By basing his ideas in the unconscious and suggesting that things are only revealed in psychoanalysis, Freud's theory is unfalsifiable and thus is not proper science.
Freud is able to explain differences in moral thinking. If conscience were the voice of God as Newman believed, then it is odd that different moral views exist. By linking our ideas of right and wrong to our varied upbringing and culture, Freud is able to explain different moral views.	Erich Fromm has argued that Freud is only partially correct about the conscience. Many people do have a conscience that is driven by a fear of punishment and authority. This does not explain the acts of those who challenge authority, however. Fromm argues that there exists a humanitarian conscience that some of us develop (see page 118).

Activities

Core

1 What does Freud mean by the unconscious?
2 Explain briefly what each of the id, ego and superego do.
3 How does Freud think that our upbringing may affect the conscience?

Stretch

4 Look at the key strengths of Freud's view of the conscience in the table. Which is the best point? Justify your answer.

5 Look at the key weaknesses of Freud's view of the conscience in the table. Which is the best point? Justify your answer.

Challenge

6 Find out more about the ego, id and superego by accessing psychology websites such as www.simplypsychology.org. Add a few key ideas or quotes to your notes.

8.3 Comparing Aquinas and Freud

Aim

Compare Aquinas' and Freud's ideas and consider which thinker best explains key aspects of the conscience.

Starter

Based on what you have learned so far, do you think Aquinas' or Freud's view of the conscience is better? Discuss in pairs and write a one or two sentence answer.

Aquinas and Freud in conversation

A useful method of studying Philosophy and Ethics is through dialogue as it allows people to engage with very different views. A problem with this method, however, is that very often the thinkers involved inhabit very different time periods. Hence we must use a little artistic licence.

Round 1: Guilt

Freud: One thing I note about your theory of conscience is that it doesn't seem to say much about guilt. I think our experience of guilt is actually crucial to the conscience. I might even go so far as to say that the conscience is guilt.

Aquinas: I think you have gone too far there. I accept that guilt is an emotion we may experience, but conscience is far more than that. Our synderesis and conscientia enable us to work out how to act. Guilt is merely a byproduct of going against what we have worked out. It is precisely because we are being irrational that we feel guilt.

Freud: You're right that we feel guilty when we go against our moral standards, but if anything is irrational it is actually the feeling of guilt itself. It is an immature response to the gap that emerges between the standards we are trying to live up to and the reality of our lives. Our parents give us impossible ideals, we fall short and guilt occurs – but it is illogical that we feel that way.

Aquinas: It's interesting that you focus on guilt. Our friend John Newman would argue that guilt implies responsibility and a being that we are responsible towards – guilt leads us to God.

Commentator: A strong round for Freud! It seems he is right that the experience of guilt is immediate rather than something that comes afterwards. It may be a matter of debate as to which thinker is right on whether guilt is rational or irrational. Something to think about and take a view on.

Round 2: God

Freud: This is another area where I believe that my view is stronger. The problem with religious views of the conscience is that you are left with the absurd view that God has told different people different things about what is right and wrong.

Aquinas: If I could stop you there, I think you are misrepresenting my view. You are right that some religious thinkers see conscience as the voice of God or as some sort of divine intuition. I agree with you that this is mistaken. Conscience does have a link to God; it is a tool that God has given us to enable us to work out what is right and wrong, hence it is perfectly possible that some may use the tool correctly and others incorrectly.

Freud: That's all very well but you need to prove the existence of God, surely? God did not create us; we created God. Ludwig Feuerbach was quite correct in suggesting that we take human characteristics and stretch them – 'God is man written in large letters', I believe he once said. God is a comfort blanket to meet our deepest psychological needs. Although the reality is that the belief is deeply psychologically damaging, particularly to our moral beliefs.

Aquinas: It strikes me that you are confusing two things – the psychological effect of religious belief and whether or not there are good reasons to believe that God exists. I would argue that God's existence can be proved in five ways, including cosmological and teleological arguments and that this world is ordered by God. That order – including the moral order – can be discovered by reason.

Freud: I think you are projecting your moral ideas on to the world rather than discovering them.

Commentator: A better round for Aquinas. He avoids some of the difficulties that other theological views get themselves into, including explaining moral differences and errors. Aquinas is right that Freud tends more to assume the non-existence of God rather than prove it. A reliance on the subconscious may also show that Freud's views cannot be falsified, although this issue also affects Aquinas.

Round 3: Making moral decisions

Aquinas: One thing that I am not clear on with regards to your view is how moral decisions are made. It seems that your focus on the unconscious takes away all reflection on moral issues.

Freud: Perhaps, but you are being a little unfair. There is no innate synderesis as in your view; we will have feelings of approval or disapproval of various actions but we are free to ignore these and choose our own actions.

Aquinas: Sorry, but I don't see how you are free at all, if all the influences are unconscious then our initial feelings and our subsequent reflections are determined for us rather than chosen. We cannot help what we feel. Contrast this with my view. I am giving people responsibility; they reason and decide what to do, they are able to educate their consciences. I don't see any responsibility in your view.

Freud: The advantages that you claim can only be the case if your whole theory is correct.

Commentator: Both thinkers make good points here. Any strengths that either thinker has would ultimately depend on their whole theory being correct. You need to decide for yourself who has the stronger arguments.

Activities

Core

1 What is the difference between Aquinas' and Freud's views of the role of guilt in conscience?
2 What is the role of God within Aquinas' view of the conscience?
3 How should we use 'conscience' in our moral decision-making, according to Freud?

Stretch

4 Which thinker's views on guilt do you think make the most sense? Write a paragraph explaining your answer.

5 Which thinker's views on moral decision-making do you think make the most sense? Write a paragraph justifying your answer.

Challenge

6 Continue the dialogue, either by considering the themes of rationality vs subconscious or by introducing a third thinker, such as Newman or Fromm.

8.4 Does conscience stem from reason or the unconscious mind?

Aim

Investigate the views of various thinkers including Aquinas and Freud on whether conscience is based on reasoning or comes from the unconscious mind.

Starter

Sort the following terms into two columns depending on whether they are used by Aquinas or Freud:

conscientia; ego; id; invincible ignorance; psychosexual development; ratio; superego; synderesis; unconscious; vincible ignorance.

If you want something a little more challenging, try to define each term as well.

Aquinas and Freud

For Aquinas, conscience is very much the product of reason. God has created us with the ability to reason and we have the awareness of moral law (synderesis) within us. We then have the responsibility to develop this and use our conscientia to apply and make moral judgements.

For Freud, conscience is not rational. It is the product of the unconscious mind. It is the internalised voice of our parents and society that is in the superego, and it attempts to restrain the inappropriate desires of the id. This inner struggle is subconscious and hidden from us.

Erich Fromm

One thinker who develops Freud's view is Erich Fromm (1900–80). Fromm does not totally agree with Freud, however. He believes that each of us has two consciences: the authoritarian conscience and the humanistic conscience. It is dependent on the individual as to which is stronger.

For most of us, the authoritarian conscience dominates; this is effectively Freud's view that conscience is about fear of authority. We internalise our feelings of fear so that our inner voice becomes that of the authority. We fear and obey the authority's rules whether they are present or absent, and regardless of whether the commands are logical. While a good authoritarian conscience gives us a sense of wellbeing and security, a bad authoritarian conscience makes obedience the supreme moral value and fear of punishment overrides all other feelings. To illustrate this point, Fromm uses the example of ordinary Germans feeling guilty about disobeying the Nazis.

Some of us, however, are able to develop a humanistic conscience. The humanistic conscience differs greatly from Freudian views. It is our own inner voice reacting to how well we are functioning in life. It is our reaction to our own behaviour, almost like looking in a mirror and asking, 'What sort of person am I?' Fromm argues that this is a higher and more developed conscience, but for many of us the authoritarian conscience dominates.

Tip

It is important to note that it is possible to address whether conscience is the product of reason or part of the unconscious mind purely with reference to Aquinas and Freud. There is no requirement to go beyond these two thinkers. However, bringing in the perspectives of other thinkers could also be an interesting way to approach such a question. Either approach is valid.

Analyse and evaluate

It could be argued that conscience stems from reason because:	*It could be argued that conscience stems from the unconscious mind because:*
Unlike other theological ideas, the appeal to reason explains the fact that moral views change over time and that moral views differ between people. It is the result of people reasoning differently.	Both Freud and Fromm seem to be correct in showing that conscience is at least in part an instinctive or subconscious reaction to authority. This does in some circumstances lead people to do things that are not logical or reasonable.
Both Piaget's theory of moral development and Fromm's humanistic conscience require an ability to reflect and assess one's attitudes and beliefs that is developed over time – at least by some of us. This would suggest that conscience cannot be totally explained by appeal to the unconscious.	If conscience is part of the unconscious mind and linked to society/upbringing then this does explain why moral ideas differ to some extent. Our minds are formed differently by our unique experiences, which become trapped in our subconscious.
By appealing to reason, we are perhaps opening up a debate about what it is to be human. For Aquinas (and Aristotle who influences him), the ability to reason is part of our unique and special human nature. For thinkers such as Freud and Dawkins, there is nothing special as such about human beings; we are just marginally more evolved than other creatures.	Freud seems to be correct in recognising that conscience feelings present themselves immediately and as such don't seem to be the product of rational reflection.

It could be argued that conscience does not stem from reason because:	*It could be argued that conscience does not stem from the unconscious mind because:*
If moral judgements really were the product of reason, surely we would expect to see more moral agreement than we currently do; it seems that moral views vary greatly between individuals and across cultures.	As Karl Popper notes, this theory is not properly based on science despite Freud's case studies. A feature of a scientific theory is that it is able to be falsified. There is no way to falsify an appeal to the unconscious.
You may wish to look at the general strengths and weaknesses of Aquinas' view on the conscience to add to these points.	You may wish to look at the general strengths and weaknesses of Freud's view on the conscience to add to these points.

Activities

Core

1 Write one to two sentences explaining Aquinas' view on this issue.
2 Write one to two sentences explaining Freud's view on this issue.
3 For a different thinker of your choice, write one or two sentences explaining their view on whether conscience stems from reason or the unconscious mind.

Stretch

4 Look at the strengths and weaknesses of Aquinas and Freud given on the previous pages. Add these to your notes where they are relevant.

5 Write a conclusion for an essay that asks you whether conscience is the product of the unconscious mind. What do you think and what is your main reason for reaching that view?

Challenge

6 Research the views of Erich Fromm on authoritarian and humanistic consciences. Which side of the debate on this page does he best fit on?

8.5 Is conscience a real thing or a label for other factors in moral decision-making?

Starter

Sort the list below into things that exist (real) and things that do not exist (not real): monsters; love; tables; trains; Harry Potter; goodness; yellow; dogs; four-sided triangles; dark matter; beauty; aliens.

Some of them, for example love and goodness, may be a matter of debate – we might wonder what 'real' means – do these terms refer to things that actually exist in the universe or are they just names/words that we use to describe phenomena?

Aim

Investigate whether conscience exists at all or is instead an umbrella term covering various factors involved in moral decision-making, such as culture, environment, genetic predisposition and education.

Aquinas and Freud

Aquinas believes that conscience is a real thing; it is a part of our human nature given to us by God. Freud does not believe that conscience is a real thing as such; it is a word that we use to describe the guilt caused by our upbringing and environment.

Conscience as real and God-given

The Bible has a number of references to conscience and seems to suggest that this is a real feature of human nature given by God. In the key quote, the Apostle Paul answers the question of how the Gentiles (non-Jews) who had not received the Old Testament law would know the difference between right and wrong. Paul's answer is to suggest that the Gentiles had a conscience regardless of access to scripture, which is the equivalent of having God's laws written 'on their hearts'. Yet this does not automatically mean that people always know what is right and wrong. Elsewhere in the New Testament, Paul warns that people can sear or damage their consciences by persistently not listening to them.

One of the more famous theological accounts of the conscience is from John Henry Newman (1801–90), who argues that conscience is the voice of God. Newman starts with our experience of conscience. It is as much a part of our psychology as memory, reason and imagination – and it would be odd if we denied the existence of one of these things. It is an indisputable fact of our psychological life. Newman argues that it is a precondition: without it, there can be no such thing as morality. Conscience is also authoritative: it doesn't just offer advice, it needs to be obeyed, as shown by the guilt, fear or shame we feel when we ignore it. Conscience feelings also imply a higher or supreme judge who can instill fear and inflict punishment. Hence the phenomena of conscience that we all experience indicates that God exists.

Conscience as an umbrella term

Conscience and genetic predispositions

Some of the more interesting recent work on conscience has come from thinkers offering evolutionary explanations of the phenomenon. Like Freud, this view rejects the idea that conscience is a real 'thing' as such; moral thinking and attitudes simply evolved. This approach is taken by Richard Dawkins (1941–). Dawkins argues that human beings are the sum total of

Tip

The two thinkers named on the specification may be a natural starting point. It is possible to consider this question solely in relation to them. Yet equally it is possible to extend to discussion of other thinkers.

Key quote

'[The Gentiles] show that the requirements of the law are written on their hearts; their consciences also bearing witness, and their thoughts sometimes accusing them and at other times even defending them.'
(Apostle Paul in Romans 2:15)

their genes; we are 'bytes and bytes of DNA'. Just as various abilities and traits are at least partly genetic, so too there is a genetic explanation for morality. Some people are more likely to act altruistically and others are not. Those humans who cooperate with their fellow creatures and help others are more likely to survive and thus pass on their 'more moral' genes than those who act purely out of selfishness. Hence, over many generations nature has effectively selected those who have these good, moral attitudes.

Conscience as culture, environment and education

Other thinkers agree that conscience is not a real thing but rather is a name for other factors, but they argue these factors are more the product of nurture rather than nature. As seen with Freud, our upbringing may be said to play a significant part in our moral views. Other thinkers, such as Jean Piaget (1896–1980), share the view that our environment and education are key to understanding the idea that we call conscience. Piaget suggests that our moral views develop through at least two distinct stages: younger children typically under 10 years old view rules as imposed by authority figures, whereas older children and adults understand that rules are things that human beings make and can change.

Analyse and evaluate

It can be argued that conscience is a real thing because:	It can be argued that conscience is merely a label or umbrella term for other factors because:
Aquinas identifies conscience as part of human nature; our ability to reason is given by God as a result of being made in his image.	Many of the explanations that conscience is a real thing rely on the existence of God.
Newman argues that it would be strange to deny the existence of conscience as it is undeniable that we experience this phenomenon. It would be equivalent to dismissing memory or imagination, *but* ... (See umbrella term argument 2)	(From real thing argument 2) ... It may well be that our experiences of conscience have a brain-based explanation and that evolution can account for conscience in just the same way as it accounts for memory and conscious thought.
You may wish to look at the general strengths and weaknesses of Aquinas' view on the conscience to add to these points.	The existence of differing moral views in varying cultures is problematic, particularly for Newman, as we should expect the voice of God to be universal.
	You may wish to look at the general strengths and weaknesses of Freud's view on the conscience to add to these points.

Activities

Core

1 In one or two sentences, explain how Aquinas would answer the question in the title of this section.

2 In one or two sentences, explain how Freud would answer the question in the title of this section.

3 What does Romans 2:15 have to say about the conscience?

Stretch

4 Which is the strongest argument for believing that the conscience is a real thing? Justify your answer.

5 Which is the strongest argument for believing that the conscience is merely an umbrella term to describe other factors in moral decision-making? Justify your answer.

Challenge

6 Find out more about Richard Dawkins' evolutionary view of the conscience. How does he use Susan Blackmore's idea of memes?

Wrap up

QUIZ

1 What word does Aquinas use to describe the principle that drives us to pursue good and avoid evil?

2 Which aspect of the human personality does Freud identify with conscience?

3 What is the difference between vincible and invincible ignorance?

4 Which thinker believes that conscience is the voice of God?

5 Fromm believes in authoritarian and _____ conscience.

6 What is the Oedipus complex?

7 Which thinker believes that conscience is based on reason?

8 Why is Freud's view held to be unfalsifiable?

9 What is the name that Aquinas gives to the process of making actual moral judgements?

10 Which thinker believes that 'conscience' can be explained by traits that are genetically inherited?

GET READY

Summarising

1 Make a copy of the grid below. Without looking at your notes, aim to fill in the boxes by making four or five points. You could further train your memory by trying to repeat the process after a couple of weeks.

Explain Aquinas (AO1)	Explain Freud (AO1)	Compare Aquinas and Freud (AO1)
Assess Aquinas (AO2)	Assess Freud (AO2)	Who is better and why? (AO2)
Is conscience based on reason?	Is conscience a result of the unconscious mind?	Is conscience real or an umbrella term?

Linking

2 You may wish to review your work on whistleblowing in business ethics. In what ways might whistleblowers appeal to conscience?

Applying

3 Make a concept map for conscience on paper or using an online concept-mapping tool such as Coggle to gain an overview of this topic. A suggested outline is shown below but you are free to use your own branches.

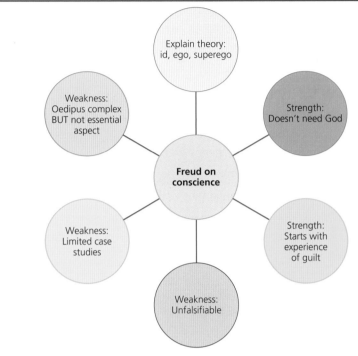

Concept map centred on **Freud on conscience** with branches:
- Explain theory: id, ego, superego
- Strength: Doesn't need God
- Strength: Starts with experience of guilt
- Weakness: Unfalsifiable
- Weakness: Limited case studies
- Weakness: Oedipus complex BUT not essential aspect

4 Using the specification and the chapter titles in this book, identify three or four possible essay questions on the conscience.

   a For each of the essays, make a concept map identifying possible points that you could raise.

   b What position would you take on each question? Use this to write your introduction and conclusion.

   c Arrange your other points into an order of paragraphs – how will you develop each point?

Debate

5 'The origin and development of conscience in a person has nothing to do with God or gods.'

Discuss this in small groups and make a note of the points raised. Add them to your notes.

Going further

6 Try writing one of the essays from Question 4 in under 40 minutes using just the plan. Ask your teacher to mark it.

 Tip

Some candidates tend to fasten all their attention to an obvious point when assessing thinkers on the conscience, for example that Aquinas relies on God or that Freud can't prove his theory. There is nothing wrong with making these points, but if the point isn't developed or if it is the only point you are making then it is very difficult to gain higher marks for assessment and evaluation as you are merely stating points.

Get practising

Ask the expert

'I noticed that some of the sample exam questions my teacher showed me used the words "critically compare". I was a bit freaked out by this because we are normally asked to assess or discuss. What would I do here?' – Shazmeen

The expert says

'Critically compare' is a command that questions may use, particularly on areas of the specification where different thinkers are specifically named, such as this one. To do this you need to do three things:

1 Think about what each thinker is saying.

2 **Compare:** What are the similarities and differences?

3 **Critically:** Argue/form a judgement as to who (if either) is right and why.

It is fair to say that better answers focus more on points 2 and 3 rather than point 1.

Shazmeen's first attempt

Aquinas believes that conscience is a tool given to us by God. We are created with the ability to reason as a result of being made in the image of God. This reasoning enables people to make good moral decisions using their synderesis and conscientia in... [the answer goes on to explain these terms]

Freud argues that conscience is the product of our subconscious; it is the guilt caused by the gap between the ideals of our parents as retained in our superego and the reality of the life we actually live. Freud's explanation does not rely on God.

This answer shows understanding of what each thinker believes so gains some AO1 marks. The question asks for comparison but the comparison here, based on God, is not clear or explicit. There is also no real critical engagement – the candidate needs to form an argument as to which view is better.

Shazmeen's improved answer

The main improvements are shown in bold.

One area where Aquinas' view of conscience makes more sense is with regards to God. Aquinas believes that conscience is a tool given to us by God. We are created with the ability to reason as a result of being made in the image of God. Aquinas refers to this as 'ratio' and it is available to all. In contrast, Freud sees no role for God, arguing that conscience is the product of our subconscious; it is the guilt caused by the gap between the ideals of our parents as retained in our superego and the reality of the life we actually live. **Yet Freud has not established the non-existence of God. His views on God represent an assumption that Feuerbach is correct in suggesting that the idea of God is a human invention. It is entirely possible that the psychological phenomenon of guilt that Freud identifies is the 'law written on our hearts' that religious thinkers identify.**

CHAPTER 9

Sexual ethics

Big picture

The topic of sexual ethics looks at a range of issues such as premarital and extramarital sex, as well as issues arising around homosexuality. Although each of the areas in this topic is legally permissible, there remain different views, particularly among the religious, regarding whether some acts may be morally wrong.

Engage

Evangelical Christian musician Vicky Beeching had been a leading performer of Christian contemporary music for almost a decade. In August 2014, she came out as gay. This produced a hostile reaction from some in the Christian community, with comments such as 'You have been deceived by the devil' being typical of the messages Vicky received on social media. Although some feel that the Bible is clear on the sinfulness of homosexuality, Vicky disagrees: 'What Jesus taught was a radical message of welcome and inclusion and love. I feel certain God loves me just the way I am, and I have a huge sense of calling to communicate that to young people.' She notes that her parents, although disagreeing with her on the theology of homosexuality, continue to love her unconditionally.

▲ Vicky Beeching came out as gay in 2014

Vicky Beeching suggests that along with sport, religion is an environment where even now it is difficult to come out as gay. What reasons might there be for this? See www.vickybeeching.com

The specification

Content	Key knowledge
<ul><li>Consideration of the following areas of sexual ethics:<ul><li>premarital and extramarital sex</li><li>homosexuality</li></ul></li><li>The influence of developments in religious beliefs and practices on debates about the morality, legality and tolerability of these areas of sexual ethics</li></ul> <ul><li>Application of the following theories to these areas of sexual ethics:<ul><li>Natural law</li><li>Situation ethics</li><li>Kantian ethics</li><li>Utilitarianism</li></ul></li></ul>	<ul><li>Traditional religious beliefs and practices (from any religious perspectives) regarding these areas of sexual ethics</li><li>How these beliefs and practices have changed over time, including:<ul><li>key teachings influencing these beliefs and practices</li><li>the ideas of religious figures and institutions</li></ul></li><li>The impact of secularism on these areas of sexual ethics</li><li>How these theories might be used to make moral decisions in these areas of sexual ethics</li><li>Issues raised in the application of these theories</li></ul>

Learners should have the opportunity to discuss issues related to ideas about sexual ethics and changing attitudes towards it, including:
- whether or not religious beliefs and practices concerning sex and relationships have a continuing role in the area of sexual ethics
- whether choices in the area of sexual behaviour should be entirely private and personal, or whether they should be subject to societal norms and legislation
- whether normative theories are useful in what they might say about sexual ethics.

9.1 Is sexual behaviour purely a private and personal matter?

Aim

Investigate whether or not there are significant ethical issues in sexual behaviour or whether sex is a purely private and personal matter.

Starter

Suppose a friend argues that sex is a private matter and has nothing to do with ethics. How might you answer them? Are there any reasons for studying the topic of sexual ethics?

Key terms

Premarital sex Sex before marriage

Extramarital sex Sex outside of marriage, where at least one party is married to someone else; also known as adultery

Contractarian The idea that moral rules or norms are based on an implicit mutual agreement, i.e. not to harm other persons (found in the philosophy of Thomas Hobbes)

Changing attitudes to sex and sexuality

Historically, society in the UK has taken much of its moral thinking from Judeo-Christian ethics, which view **premarital sex**, **extramarital sex** and homosexual relationships as falling short of God's ideal. These attitudes are changing significantly, however. The arrival of more effective forms of contraception has made premarital sex less risky than in previous generations, and the British Social Attitudes Survey 2019 (BSA 2019) found that 75 per cent of people saw no moral issues at all with premarital sex. Although homophobia remains an issue, attitudes to homosexuality are changing; gay marriage was legalised in England and Wales in 2014 and the majority of people (68 per cent) now do not consider homosexual relationships to be wrong (BSA 2019). Yet surveys suggest that people in the UK are consistent in their disapproval of extramarital sex, with around 85 per cent of people still considering it always to be wrong (Office for National Statistics Survey 2013).

One significant change in sexual behaviour has been the increase in couples who cohabit (live together) before or instead of marriage. Most couples cohabit before marrying, although according to UK census data there is statistical evidence that when cohabiting couples do go on to marry, they are more likely to divorce than those who did not cohabit.

The non-harm principle

A number of philosophers and ethicists do not feel that sexual ethics is a particularly significant ethical topic. They argue that sexuality and sexual behaviour is personal and private, and that there are no genuine or important ethical debates to be had.

Support for this claim comes from the work of John Stuart Mill (1806–73). Mill's liberalism meant he believed that governments should intervene in people's lives as little as possible. Rules are needed only in order to prevent people being harmed and to take action if harm takes place. This is known as the non-harm principle or the **contractarian** view. In terms of sexual ethics, this means that provided the people involved in the sexual behaviour have given consent and no one is being harmed, no further rules are needed. Modern utilitarian John Harris supports this view; he argues that sexual ethics as such is not needed, since issues such as violence, abuse or paedophilia would be dealt with under other ethical debates.

Foucault and feminism

Two further perspectives might challenge the thinking that sexual ethics is not a topic where there are urgent debates.

1 French philosopher Michel Foucault (1926–84) challenges religious thinking on sexual ethics as it tends to categorise sexual behaviour in terms of normal and abnormal. This unhelpful way of seeing the world needs to be challenged and rejected.

2 Feminists would also argue that sexual ethics is an important topic of discussion. Gender inequality means that women are disproportionately affected by sexual discrimination; women are more likely than men to be judged as promiscuous if they have had several partners. The #MeToo movement has also highlighted issues – including sexual abuse, assault in the workplace and the threat of revenge porn – where women are significantly more likely to be affected than men.

Analyse and evaluate

Sexual behaviour may be seen as purely a private and personal matter because:	Sexual behaviour may not be seen as just a private and personal matter because:
The contractarian view of sex argues that provided consent is present, there are no other ethical considerations that need to be satisfied. This would rule out actions considered abhorrent, such as paedophilia and rape, but would ensure freedom in other cases.	Sexual behaviour, like other areas of human life, affects people for better or worse. In the case of extramarital affairs, partners and children may be affected, hence it is not the case to say that there are no ethical concerns to discuss.
Mill's principle on non-harm would also ensure that neither politicians nor philosophers need to consider sexual matters.	Ethical theories offer a response to the contractarian or minimal view, which tends to cheapen and reduce the importance of sex. Fletcher's focus on love and Kant's respect for persons are important challenges to modern thinking.
Existentialists argue that the mistake in religious philosophy such as Aquinas' natural law is in assuming that all persons and acts have a purpose. When the idea of purpose is removed, it is possible to see sexual behaviour as purely free and personal choices.	While there are gender inequalities as discussed above, there is a need to discuss ethical issues arising from the imbalance of power within sexual relationships.

Activities

Core

1 How have social attitudes to sex and sexuality changed in recent years?

2 What is the non-harm principle?

3 Why do some thinkers argue that sexual behaviour is purely private and personal?

Stretch

4 Rank the arguments in favour of sex being understood as personal and private. Which is the strongest argument? Justify your decision.

5 Rank the arguments against sex being understood as personal and private. Which is the strongest argument? Justify your decision.

Challenge

6 Research the thoughts of Michael Foucault and add to your notes on this topic.

9.2 Is natural law a helpful approach to sexual ethics?

▲ Natural law ethics has had a significant impact on past UK laws on issues such as homosexuality. Alan Turing (1912–54), part of the group that cracked the Nazi Enigma code, committed suicide after being convicted of 'gross indecency' for his sexual relationship with another man, at a time when homosexuality was illegal

Applying natural law

Aquinas

For Aquinas, each person and each activity in the world has purpose or *telos*. The primary precepts show that one of the key purposes of human beings is reproduction, and equally when the sexual organs are considered it seems obvious to Aquinas that their purpose is to reproduce. Thus, any sexual act where reproduction is not possible does not achieve its *telos*. This logically leads to secondary precepts that rule out homosexual acts, masturbation and artificial contraception.

Aquinas believes that marriage is fundamentally important; it is a means of achieving an ordered society. For Aquinas, there are two functions or purposes of marriage: the 'generative' (bringing new life) and the 'unitive' (bringing the couple together). These purposes cannot be separated. This has influenced Roman Catholic thought in particular and is key to understanding the Catechism and various papal documents, such as Humanae vitae.

Key quote

'The fundamental nature of the marriage act, while uniting husband and wife in the closest intimacy, also renders them capable of generating new life – and this as a result of laws written into the actual nature of man and of woman.'
(Pope Paul VI, *Humanae vitae*, Chapter 12)

Due to the importance of marriage, both premarital and extramarital sex are rejected – even though reproduction is possible in these circumstances. The generation of new life should take place within marriage as this is one of its purposes. In addition, in the case of extramarital sex, the divine law through one of the Ten Commandments makes it very clear that adultery is morally wrong.

John Finnis

One modern natural law philosopher who has written on sexual ethics is John Finnis (1940–). Finnis bases his natural law thinking on the ideas of Aristotle rather than Aquinas and argues that certain things in life are basic goods of human flourishing, such as reproduction, knowledge, work, friendship and spirituality. He argues that marriage is also a basic good as it is only in marriage that both friendship and reproduction can be combined. On homosexuality, he argues that the giving of life cannot be achieved and thus homosexual sex is instrumental and harmful. A petition by students at Oxford University sought to prevent Finnis teaching at the university as a result of concern over his writings on homosexuality.

Analyse and evaluate

Natural law is a helpful approach to sexual ethics because:	Natural law is not a helpful approach to sexual ethics because:
In focusing on marriage and on reproduction, natural law avoids cheapening the sexual act, which is a consequence of some more liberal modern views.	Natural law is derived from divine law and some of the primary precepts also rely on the idea of God. If God does not exist then it can be argued that there is no ultimate reason to follow the precepts on sexuality. The theologian Hugo Grotius, however, argues that natural law is built into the universe and would apply even in the absence of God.
The focus on purpose or *telos* is helpful provided it is disentangled from some of the more legalistic interpretations that the Church has placed on it. If one of the main purposes of sex is unitive, then this can be a helpful moral principle to consider acts by.	The idea of *telos* is problematic for two reasons. Firstly, it assumes that persons have a *telos* and that this *telos* is specifically the things that Aquinas suggests. Secondly, there are assumptions about the *telos* of sexual acts – that they are generative and unitive. It could equally be argued that the *telos* of such acts is pleasure.
Natural law may be right to link marriage and the production of children. There is some statistical evidence that suggests the children of married parents are more likely to flourish in education. It could be argued that a stable environment for raising children is an important contribution that natural law makes to this debate.	Natural law argues that these ideas are part of nature and are built in to us. However, while sexual urges may be natural, not everyone has heterosexual inclinations. Homosexuality is part of some people's nature. Similarly, the theory commits the naturalistic fallacy in assuming that just because something is natural, it is automatically good.
	Natural law's focus on reproduction renders some sexual acts, such as sex between people who are infertile or elderly, as pointless.
	Natural law, particularly when interpreted through Church teaching, is legalistic and has not moved with the times, particularly where technology exists to address some of the issues highlighted, such as reproductive technologies.

Activities

Core

1 What are the two key purposes of marriage according to Aquinas?
2 Why are premarital and extramarital sex seen as wrong in natural law?
3 What does natural law teach about homosexuality?

Stretch

4 Why might critics of natural law have a problem with the idea of *telos*?

5 What is the naturalistic fallacy and how does natural law commit this fallacy with regard to sexual ethics?

Challenge

6 Pope Paul VI's Humanae vitae is widely available online. Read Sections 9–14 to get a sense of how natural law can be applied to sex and marriage. Add some key ideas or quotes to your notes.

9.3 Is situation ethics a helpful approach to sexual ethics?

 Aim

Learn how the theory of situation ethics can be applied to sexual ethics and consider how helpful this approach is.

 Starter

In pairs, review the theory of situation ethics. What is the key principle? How many of the four working principles and six propositions can you remember?

Applying situation ethics

Situation ethics (see Chapter 2) is associated with Joseph Fletcher (1905–91). For Fletcher, the key to Christian ethics is the principle of *agape* love, which is applied individually to each situation. Fletcher argues that *agape* is a middle ground between religious legalism (having too many laws), and antinomianism (having no laws or rules at all).

For Fletcher, premarital sex and homosexuality are not morally wrong provided that the acts are based on love. Even extramarital sex in some circumstances could be supported despite the specific commandment given in the Bible. Fletcher supports the decriminalisation of homosexuality, and one of his main issues with traditional religious ethics such as natural law is that its attitude to homosexuality is obviously incorrect.

Although Fletcher is relatively liberal in his approach, he warns of the danger of promiscuity. When individuals behave promiscuously, they are ignoring the value and dignity of persons and are treating them as 'love objects'.

 Key quote

'Jesus said nothing about homosexuality. Whether any form of sex (hetero, homo, or auto) is good or evil, depends fully on whether love is fully served.'
(Joseph Fletcher, *Situation Ethics: The new morality*)

▲ These Christians would agree with Fletcher that religious rules on homosexuality are outdated

Difficult cases

In *Situation Ethics*, Fletcher provides two real cases where he suggests that extramarital sex could be seen as acceptable.

1   In the Second World War, a German woman Mrs Bergmeier was captured by the Russians and held as a prisoner of war. She desperately missed her family and was concerned about their safety. Women were only released from the camp if they were pregnant. A sympathetic Russian guard offered to help her get back home. She became pregnant with his child and when the family was reunited, they raised the child as if it was their own. (See page 15.)

2 A female American agent was asked to use her sexuality to trap an enemy agent and gain information that could save lives. When she protested that she was not sure she could compromise her integrity in this way, she was told that it was no different from her brother risking his life on the front line in Korea and that they were sure they could not get the information any other way. Fletcher seems to suggest that it would be her decision to make, but if she did agree it would not be morally wrong.

Analyse and evaluate

Situation ethics is a good approach to sexual ethics because:	Situation ethics is a poor approach to sexual ethics because:
Situation ethics is person-centred, which is exactly the right approach for issues around sexuality. It is important that people come before rules in this topic.	Situation ethics overlooks the fact that there may well be absolutes in sexual ethics. Certainly from a religious perspective, the commandment 'Do not commit adultery' is clear and it is difficult to see how an exception can be made.
Situation ethics is flexible but avoids cheapening sex or allowing sex to be casual. This avoids the potential pitfall of other relativist theories such as utilitarianism, where pleasure becomes more important than the unitive aspects that are present in loving relationships.	Following on from this, in attempting to base its key principle on the ideas of Jesus, situation ethics is guilty of selective interpretation of the Bible. Love is not the sole teaching of Jesus, even if it is the most important. Jesus is very clear about issues such as divorce, for example.
Situation ethics enables decisions to be based on core religious principles yet still be flexible to the changing nature of society, particularly in terms of attitudes to cohabitation and homosexuality.	It is difficult to know how far to take the idea of love in terms of measuring consequences. Should decisions about what is most loving include children who are affected, families who may disapprove of the relationship, etc.?
Situation ethics treats people as adults and gives them the responsibility to make decisions for themselves on how *agape* is best served. External authorities such as the Church are not required.	While it may be good to some extent to place decision-making in the hands of the individual, this may prove too demanding for many people, who want to be given more guidance than the theory seems to provide.
There has often been a lack of love and mercy in religious responses to sexual ethics. Situation ethics follows the example of Jesus, who refused to condemn the woman caught in adultery (John 8:1–11).	There is a sense that the theory arrives at the idea of *agape* because of difficult cases such as that of Mrs Bergmeier. These cases are rare exceptions and it may be unwise to use them to make general rules.

Activities

Core

1 What does Fletcher believe about homosexuality? Why does he come to this view?

2 According to Fletcher, why is promiscuity dangerous?

3 'Do not commit adultery.' What would Fletcher's view of this commandment be?

Stretch

4 Look at the strengths of the theory when applied to sexual ethics. Which strength is most persuasive? Justify your answer.

5 Look at the weaknesses of the theory when applied to sexual ethics. Which weakness is most persuasive? Justify your answer.

Challenge

6 Read the Appendix of Fletcher's *Situation Ethics*. It contains the two difficult cases addressed in this chapter described in Fletcher's own words.

9.4 Should religious ideas continue to have an influence on issues in sexual ethics?

Aim

Investigate the influence of religious teachings on sexual ethics and consider whether they should continue to have an influence.

Starter

Some parents and faith groups have expressed concern about primary school children being taught about homosexuality at too young an age. They argue that it is against their faith. Sexual orientation and religious belief are both protected characteristics in terms of equality and human rights. What should happen when they clash?

Key quotes

'I tell you anyone who divorces his wife, except for sexual immorality, makes her the victim of adultery and anyone who marries a divorced woman commits adultery.' (Jesus in Matthew 5:32)

'Do you not know that wrongdoers will not inherit the kingdom of God? Do not be deceived: Neither the sexually immoral nor idolaters nor adulterers nor men who have sex with men... will inherit the Kingdom of God.' (Paul in 1 Corinthians 6:10)

'Marriage should be honoured by all, and the marriage bed kept pure, for God will judge the adulterer and all the sexually immoral.' (Hebrews 13:4)

Ancient views on sexual ethics

In order to understand the impact of religious views, it is worth asking what attitudes to sex and sexuality were like before the rise of Christianity and Islam. Greek philosophers held varying views, with Pythagoreans (followers of Pythagoras) and Plato viewing the soul as more important than the body and thus seeing sex as something corrupt. Stoic philosophers linked sex with reproduction and thus it was a necessary evil. This line of thought influenced some early Christians such as Augustine. Other philosophers such as the Cynics saw sex as something to be celebrated and public orgies were not uncommon. Sexual acts were also at times used as part of ritual worship in some cults and religious groups. It is debatable to what extent these philosophical ideas impacted the lives of the average citizen of Greece or Rome, however. Society was patriarchal and homosexuality was not unusual among educated Greeks; indeed, a sexual relationship between an older and a younger man was encouraged.

Christianity and sexual ethics

This section looks at Christianity in order to draw on previous knowledge gained when covering natural law and situation ethics. However, there is no specific requirement in the specification that the religious views need be confined to Christianity.

In terms of biblical material, Jesus says very little about sexuality. The only text that has any relevance is his condemnation of divorce (see key quote). The Apostle Paul, who writes much of the New Testament, argues that Christians should remain celibate – he believes that the end of the world is imminent but that Christians can marry if they are unable to control their passions! He also seems to condemn homosexuality and adultery (see key quote), however there is some debate as to whether the word translated as 'homosexual' actually means this or whether it refers to male prostitution.

How much weight should be attached to the biblical material may depend upon the different approaches that Christians take:

- A Roman Catholic Christian may give equal weight to Church teaching, natural law ethics and the biblical material.
- A liberal Christian may value the Bible but not feel the need to interpret and apply Paul's teaching literally.
- An evangelical Christian may take the biblical teaching more in its literal sense.

Homosexuality – an example

For Christians, the issues surrounding homosexuality are not just about gay sex. They extend to whether gay marriage, although legal, can be supported, whether gay couples should be allowed to adopt children and how far Christians who oppose homosexuality can go in expressing legitimate criticism.

A broad spectrum exists among Christians in terms of attitudes to homosexuality, as shown by the diagram below.

Sees homosexual acts as an unforgivable sin.	Sees homosexual acts as sinful but no more sinful than other sinful acts.	Believes the act may be sinful but the inclination is not. It needs to be resisted and celibacy is required.	Theologically unsure – sees the complexity of the arguments on both sides.	Does not see homosexuality as sinful but stops short of supporting gay marriage – biblical marriage is male and female.	Supports full equality – views biblical texts as outdated.

Analyse and evaluate

Religious ideas should not continue to have an influence on sexual ethics because:	*Religious ideas should continue to have an influence on sexual ethics because:*
Society has changed in its attitudes both to religion and to sexuality. Given that less than half the population believe in God, it seems strange that religious beliefs should dominate.	Religious ideas are a useful contrast to a modern culture that risks cheapening sex and approaching the topic with a consumer mindset rather than seeing the value of persons and relationships.
Mill's non-harm principle and the requirement for consent seem to address most of the difficulties that arise in sexual ethics. There is no need for any extra principles from religion.	Historically, religious ideas have been enlightened when understood in their context. Jesus' teaching on divorce does not distinguish between genders, and the teaching of Muhammad (PBUH) does much to challenge the culture of his time in terms of attitudes to women and sex.
Some religious attitudes, particularly natural law with its narrow focus on reproduction, are not only outdated but also fail to understand the importance of sex.	Marriage is valued in religion and there is statistical evidence that marriage has benefits in terms of overall wellbeing and life chances of any children produced compared to those who are not brought up within marriage.
Foucault argues that religious ethics have introduced the unhelpful ideas of normal and abnormal into this topic.	

Activities

Core

1 What does Jesus teach about sexual ethics?
2 What are Paul's views about homosexuality and adultery?
3 What issues are there for Christians around the topic of homosexuality?

Stretch

4 What are the difficulties in understanding and applying biblical material on sexual ethics?

5 How have some Christian philosophers used the ideas of Pythagoras and Plato to develop their thinking?

Challenge

6 In order to gain a contrast to the Judeo-Christian views on this topic, research the attitudes of the ancient Greeks to sex and sexuality.

9.5 Is Kantian ethics a helpful approach to sexual ethics?

Aim

Learn how Kantian ethics can be applied to sexual ethics and consider how helpful this approach is.

Starter

Review the topic of Kantian ethics by copying and completing the table from the top of the page.

Key term	Explanation
Categorical imperative	
Hypothetical imperative	
Universal law	
Persons as ends	

Understanding Kant – persons and marriage

To understand Kant's views on sexual ethics, it is important to return to the idea of persons. As humans we are 'persons' due to our ability to make free and rational decisions. We have desires (as do animals) but we are unique in having 'will' – the ability to make rational decisions about our desires. Although we may desire a portion of chips, we are able to make a rational decision that overrides that desire if we are dieting or have already eaten a meal. A dog or cat cannot do this as they just have desires. Kant's main concern about sexuality is that it can reduce us purely to acting on desires; we are literally reduced to the level of animals.

This can be avoided in marriage. Marriage does not degrade us as persons because the couple has freely and rationally chosen to enter into a contract with each other. It is in effect a giving and receiving of persons. In this context, a sexual relationship can be based both on will and desire.

Applying Kantian ethics

Kantian ethics can be applied to the issues of premarital and extramarital sex and homosexuality:

- **Premarital sex:** Kant would oppose premarital sex as it is not based on the mutual promise-making that is offered in marriage. In addition, sex risks being based on animal instincts and lusts. For Kant this would be the case for all premarital sex, but it is arguably particularly the case for one-night stands and more casual encounters.

- **Extramarital sex:** For Kant, extramarital sex would break the promises that were made in the marriage ceremony and this promise-breaking cannot be universalised. In addition, it is impossible to engage in extramarital sex without treating at least one if not both of the parties involved as a means to an end.

- **Homosexuality:** Kant himself is opposed to homosexuality. He sees it as a degradation of human nature based purely on desire, which means that it is not possible to treat the other person as an end. In addition, it could

> ## Key quote
>
> 'Taken by itself [erotic love] is a degradation of human nature. But it can be expressed with reciprocity in the monogamous lifelong union of married life where it reestablishes the rational personality.'
> (Immanuel Kant, *Lectures on Ethics*)

be argued that homosexuality cannot be universalised as this would lead to the human race dying out. Modern Kantians do not necessarily share Kant's view here. They would argue that given that someone's sexuality is part of their identity, homosexual relationships (particularly marriage) should be permitted as this allows the persons involved to be treated 'as an end' rather than as a means to an end.

Developing Kant's ideas

While many modern supporters of Kantian ethics would agree with his views, other neo-Kantians would suggest that his views are too dependent on the concept of marriage. It may be possible if both parties are in agreement in almost a 'contract-based way' to allow premarital sex including one-night stands and prostitution as they wouldn't necessarily be treating the other as an end. However, it is important to note that Kant himself would strongly disagree with such a development

Analyse and evaluate

Kantian ethics is a helpful approach to sexual ethics because:	Kantian ethics is not a helpful approach to sexual ethics because:
Respect for persons is a useful feature of Kantian ethics; ensuring we treat people as persons and not as objects is a principle that it is hard to disagree with.	The principle of universal law is an odd one to apply to sexual ethics. While Kant is right that the human race would die out if everyone only had homosexual sex, he is wrong in that not everyone desires this. It is perfectly possible in a society such as ours, where less than one in ten people will have homosexual relationships.
Kantian ethics achieves the rare combination of giving some clear rules while not relying on religion. The secular nature of Kantian ethics is particularly helpful in an age when people are less religious.	Kant's optimism about marriage may be misplaced. Over 40 per cent of marriages end in divorce and feminist writers such as Simone de Beauvoir argue that the institution of marriage enslaves women and takes away their freedom.
Kantian ethics is based on logic and rational principles. This is important in a topic such as this where emotion can cloud judgement, *but* ... (See opposite)	(See opposite) ... Kant's rationality is oddly out of place in this topic. Arguably, emotions and passions are at the heart of this topic and to suggest an ethical system that dismisses these seems to dismiss a key aspect of our humanity.

Activities

Core

1 Why does Kant think that marriage is important?
2 Why is the concept of persons important to Kant on this issue? (Hint: will and desire.)
3 Why does Kant oppose extramarital sex?

Stretch

4 Write a paragraph explaining the different views Kantians may have on homosexuality.

5 Look at the arguments for and against the Kantian approach. Which argument do you consider to be the strongest? Justify your answer.

Challenge

6 Research some modern Kantian views on sexual ethics. Add this information to your notes.

9.6 Is utilitarianism a helpful approach to sexual ethics?

Aim

Learn how utilitarianism can be applied to sexual ethics and consider how helpful this approach is.

Starter

Review utilitarianism by writing a paragraph of around 100 words. You should use the terms relative, teleological, act, rule and hedonic calculus, and explain these terms as you write.

Understanding utilitarianism

Pleasure, non-harm, and challenging the topic

Utilitarianism is a relativist and teleological theory of ethics. Act utilitarians such as Bentham would approach sexual ethics on a case-by-case basis. Key to Bentham's views on this and other topics is the idea of pleasure. Whatever brings the most pleasure is the right action. For utilitarians, pleasure is the key purpose of sex and the idea found in natural law that sex is only for procreation is rejected.

John Stuart Mill would identify sex as a lower pleasure compared to some of the more important intellectual and social pleasures. The role of sex within a relationship in terms of uniting a couple may be considered. He also held a liberal attitude towards sex and his non-harm principle – that governments should not intervene or make laws unless someone is harming someone else – is applied here. This has meant that utilitarians have been tolerant of various sexual practices provided consent is involved.

More modern utilitarians, such as John Harris and Peter Singer, have questioned whether ethical discussion is required on this topic. They argue that there are no unique moral issues in sexual ethics as the moral issues that may arise – honesty, concern for others, etc. – are dealt with elsewhere. Singer has argued that there are greater and more important moral questions that arise from driving a car, such as the effect on the environment and the potential to harm others.

Applying utilitarianism

Utilitarianism can be applied to the issues of premarital and extramarital sex and homosexuality:

- **Premarital sex:** Utilitarians would ordinarily not have any issues with premarital sex. This is particularly true now that better access to contraception prevents some of the negative consequences of sex, such as unwanted pregnancies and sexually transmitted diseases. Mill was an active campaigner for better contraception among the poor as overpopulation causes more pain and misery.

- **Extramarital sex:** Utilitarians may have reasons to oppose extramarital sex on the grounds the pain and harm it may cause outweighs any initial pleasure, yet this would be judged on a case-by-case basis. Philosopher Richard Taylor, in his book *Having Love Affairs* argues that passionate love is one of life's greatest goods and that there is nothing wrong in either having affairs or, if necessary, concealing the affair in order to prevent harm to another. Some rule utilitarians may argue that the non-harm principle might lead to the opposite point, however, as affairs would typically cause more harm than good.

- **Homosexuality:** Both Bentham and Mill were progressive in their approach to homosexuality, arguing that there was no logical reason for the law that at the time made homosexual acts a criminal offence. Modern preference utilitarians, such as Peter Singer would reject the idea that homosexuality causes some people offence; people should be free to pursue the things that bring them pleasure or joy in life, whatever they are, so long as this does not harm anyone else.

One factor that is worth noting about utilitarianism is that the theory is open to evidence and its views can be changed accordingly. Once it is established that homosexuality does not corrupt character or cause illness then the utilitarian must change their view accordingly. Likewise, if evidence shows that married people are happier and their children statistically do better at school. If it could be proved that there is a clear causal link – rather than just a correlation – then the utilitarians would have to change their views about marriage and cohabitation to match the evidence.

Analyse and evaluate

Utilitarianism is a helpful approach to sexual ethics because:	Utilitarianism is not a helpful approach to sexual ethics because:
Utilitarianism is modern and progressive. Its views on topics such as homosexuality and cohabitation were ahead of their time and society has now caught up with the utilitarian ideas.	Bentham's utilitarianism focuses on the pleasure of the majority and, as its critics have famously observed, is a swine ethic. There is no reason why gang rape would count as wrong if Bentham's ethics were applied. Admittedly this is less of an issue for Mill's or Singer's version of utilitarianism.
Similarly, it is a secular theory that recognises that the traditional way of thinking about some topics in sexual ethics is based on religion and needs to be replaced by a way of thinking that does not rely on religious standards.	Basing decisions on pleasure is not a solid basis for ethical reasoning. Our emotions change; we may come to regret and see as painful an encounter that we considered pleasurable at the time. When our passions are involved, it is difficult for us to objectively consider pleasure and pain, and weigh consequences.
Utilitarianism is flexible to the situation and has minimal rules. This is significant as it can be argued that sex is mostly a personal and private matter, which requires in Mill's words a 'minimal morality'. Yet utilitarianism is not a laissez-faire ethic and it does judge acts where others are harmed as wrong, for example rape or forced prostitution.	Mill recognises that one potential problem of utilitarianism is the 'tyranny of the majority', where minority views of what may constitute pleasure may be suppressed. This could lead to either homophobic laws or the banning of religious criticism of homosexuality, depending on what the majority view may be.
	Utilitarianism states that consequences that are often outside our control dictate whether something is right or wrong. This does not make sense. It seems odd to say that the same act – that of having an affair – is either good or bad depending on whether one's spouse finds out.

Activities

Core
1 What is the key purpose of sex according to utilitarians?
2 How do Bentham and Mill argue in favour of permitting homosexuality?
3 What do John Harris and Peter Singer think about sexual ethics?

Stretch
4 Write a paragraph explaining how utilitarians may differ on the issue of extramarital sex.

5 Look at the arguments for and against the utilitarian approach to sexual ethics. Which argument do you consider to be the strongest? Justify your answer.

Challenge
6 Utilitarians are interested in evidence that may suggest which actions/institutions may cause greater good or harm. What is the evidence that marriage benefits individuals and society?

9.7 The Big Debate: Are deontological approaches to sexual ethics better than teleological approaches?

Starter

Make a copy of the table below. Working with a partner, try to fill in each box by applying the ethical theory to the issues.

Aim

Draw together everything that has been discussed in this chapter and use it to consider whether the deontological ethical theories (natural law, Kantian ethics) are better than the teleological ethical theories (utilitarianism, situation ethics) in dealing with issues in sexual ethics. When you have heard both sides of the case, you decide the outcome.

	Utilitarianism	Kantian ethics	Natural law	Situation ethics
Premarital sex				
Extramarital sex				
Homosexuality				

Preparing the case

Do the ethical theories provide help when dealing with issues in sexual ethics? Are the deontological theories, which tend to be more absolute, more helpful than the teleological theories, which tend to take a more relative approach to the issues?

The case for the prosecution

Deontological approaches to sexual ethics are better than teleological approaches

Evidence for deontological approaches being better might include the following thinkers or ideas:

Thomas Aquinas: Primary precepts include reproduction; this is the *telos* of all sexual activity. These prevent the misuse of sex.

John Finnis: There are basic facts about what leads to human flourishing. Marriage is a basic human good and is the proper place for sexual activity.

Immanuel Kant: The requirement that we treat others as an end rather than as a means to an end ensures that people are treated with proper respect and not used to satisfy the lusts of others.

The case for the defence

Deontological approaches to sexual ethics are not better; teleological approaches are better

Evidence against deontological views on sexual ethics might include the following thinkers/ideas:

> **Jeremy Bentham:** It is important to base decisions on sexual ethics on individual cases rather than rules. What is likely to lead to more pleasure and less pain?

> **J.S. Mill:** The non-harm principle allows flexibility and prevents unnecessary rules being made. (This led Mill to support the decriminalisation of homosexuality.)

> **Joseph Fletcher:** The problem with deontological views is that they are too legalistic. It is important to focus on people rather than rules, particularly in an area such as sexual ethics.

I'll see you in court

You can work through the process below individually either verbally or in written form (sometimes verbalising thoughts is the first step to being able to write them down), or you could work through the activities as a group or class, debating and reaching a verdict.

The judge opens the case: What do different deontological and teleological ethical theories suggest about premarital sex, extramarital sex and homosexuality?

↓

The case for the prosecution is presented: Deontological approaches to sexual ethics are helpful. What are the key arguments in favour of this view? What key evidence would be presented?

↓

Defence cross-examination: What are the issues arising from this evidence? What counterarguments can be brought forward?

↓

The case for the defence is presented: Deontological views are not helpful. What are the key arguments against these theories? What key evidence would be presented?

→

Prosecution cross-examination: What are the issues arising from this evidence? What counterarguments can be brought forward?

↓

Closing speeches: What is the key piece of evidence for the prosecution case?
What is the key piece of evidence for the defence case?

↓

Jury decision: What conclusion do you reach? Why? (If you are doing this exercise as a class/group you can take a vote.)

Activities

Core

1 Create a large concept map that outlines the case in favour of deontological approaches to sexual ethics.

2 Create a large concept map that outlines the case in favour of teleological approaches to sexual ethics.

3 Write a speech to use in the court case – select one of the arguments or scholars. Make your speech persuasive by adding justified reasons and examples to support your view.

Stretch

4 Write questions to ask the defence and prosecution witnesses. Make them as tricky as possible.

5 Think about possible answers to your questions – how could you respond and challenge the witness further? (This is developing the skill of critical analysis found in AO2 Level 6.)

Challenge

6 'We don't need ethical theories when it comes to the issues around the ethics of sex, we just need common sense.' How would you respond to this? Use the information on this spread to plan an answer and draw up a conclusion.

Wrap up

QUIZ

1 Which principle from John Stuart Mill is often applied in this topic?
2 What do natural law thinkers believe to be the main purpose of sex?
3 What is the main purpose of sex according to utilitarians?
4 Who argues that erotic love has the potential to degrade human nature?
5 What do the words generative and unitive mean?
6 What does Jesus have to say about homosexuality?
7 What does the divine law say about sexual ethics?
8 What does situation ethics have to say about premarital sex?
9 Which nineteenth-century philosophers argued for the legalisation of homosexuality?
10 In what year was gay marriage legalised?

GET READY

Summarising

1 Look at the four quotes below. Match them up with the four ethical theories.

Natural law	'The main purpose of sex is pleasure. This means that provided adults give consent, there isn't really any form of sexual activity that can be counted as wrong. There doesn't need to be any rules other than this.'
Situation ethics	'The main purpose of sex is reproduction. This is one of the main functions of human beings and is key to their flourishing. This means that any sexual activity that is not able to lead to reproduction falls short of this ideal.'
Kantian ethics	'It is important to retain the link between sex and marriage. It is only in marriage that people are able to treat each other with the dignity and respect that persons deserve. If there is no marriage then sex risks treating the other person as if they were an object.'
Utilitarianism	'Some of the traditional religious rules on sex and marriage are outdated. What matters is whether it is based on achieving a positive and loving outcome. Both heterosexual and homosexual relationships can demonstrate love.'

Linking

2 This topic is an excellent chance to review past topics on the ethical theories. Look through your notes on the strengths and weaknesses of the different ethical theories and make a list of which ones might apply to sexual ethics. Practise writing a few paragraphs applying these points.

 Tip

Candidates sometimes assume that applying an ethical theory to sexual ethics is AO2 – it is not; you are still demonstrating knowledge and understanding (AO1). AO2 is about assessment and evaluation – how good the ethical theory is at dealing with the issues.

Debate

3 'The right to freely express one's identity is more important than a religious believer's right to free speech.'
Make a note of points that are raised in this quote. Consider how you might use them in an essay on sexual ethics.

Going further

4 The Bible and homosexuality: Using the internet, look up some of the different biblical passages used to argue about homosexuality and see how different organisations and theologians interpret them.

CHECKLIST

I know, understand and can ...

☐ explain issues arising from premarital and extramarital sex

☐ explain some of the issues surrounding homosexuality

☐ explain how religious attitudes to sex and sexuality have developed and influenced thinking in this area

☐ explain how the four ethical theories (natural law, situation ethics, Kantian ethics, utilitarianism) can be applied to help make decisions regarding sexual ethics

☐ consider the extent to which each of the ethical theories (natural law, situation ethics, Kantian ethics, utilitarianism) is helpful in its responses to sexual ethics

☐ assess whether religious views still have a role in modern sexual ethics

☐ assess whether sexual behaviour is private or whether it is a matter for ethical and legal discussion.

Get practising

Ask the expert

'I never plan my essays but I've started to think that I should as my marks haven't been great and my teacher wants me to plan. However, my friend writes really detailed plans – sometimes a page long – but his marks are not much better than mine. What should I do?' – Alex

The expert says

The truth is somewhere between the two of you. Where candidates don't plan at all, essays run the risk of being unstructured and wandering off the question. Equally, don't spend too long planning as this eats into your writing time. Planning is for your benefit only – you won't get marks for your plan.

Spend two or three minutes thinking and identifying your main points – all you need is what your four or five main points will be and how you will develop them. This leaves over 35 minutes to write. Three minutes planning and 35 minutes writing will always be better than 40 minutes flat-out writing.

Alex's improved essay plan

NL not best

P1 – NL assumes purpose/*telos* – too much emphasis on reproduction; utilitarianism gives different purpose; existentialism no purpose

P2 – NL assumes heterosexuality 'natural' – no evidence + Foucault normal/abnormal; utilitarianism better

P3 – NL values marriage – evidence may support, not all marriages 'loving'; situation ethics better

P4 – NL supports Christian view – divine law – but legalistic RC interpretation not loving; situation ethics better

NL not best

 Tip

One of the main issues that causes problems in exams is a failure to answer the question that has been set. Candidates look at a question, see a key phrase such as 'sexual ethics' and instantly launch into their pre-prepared answer – often at length! It is worth remembering that Level 2 of the mark scheme talks about focusing on the general topic rather than the specific question set. You can avoid this by BUGging the question:

B **Box** the command word – what are you being asked to do?

U **Underline** any key words so that you don't miss anything obvious.

G **Glance** quickly through the question again to ensure you haven't missed anything.

Glossary

Absolutism In ethics, the idea that right and wrong is fixed at all times and for all people

Act utilitarianism The idea that we should always perform the act that leads to the greatest balance of good over evil

Active euthanasia A treatment is given that directly causes the death of the individual

Antinomianism Having no rules or laws at all

Autonomy Literally 'self-ruling'; the belief that we are free and able to make our own decisions

Capitalism An economic system based on private ownership and free trade rather than government intervention

Categorical imperative A command that is good in itself regardless of consequences

Cognitive The belief that moral statements are able to be true or false

Conscientia A person's reason making moral judgements

Consumerism A belief in the importance of acquiring material things

Corporate social responsibility The idea that a business has responsibilities towards the community and environment (all stakeholders)

Deontological An ethic that is focused on the rightness or wrongness of the action itself

Double effect The idea that if doing something good also produces a bad side-effect, it is still ethically permissible as the bad side-effect was not intended

Duty Acting morally according to the good, regardless of consequences

Ego The part of our personality that mediates between the id and the demands of social interaction

Emotivism The belief that ethical terms evince (show) approval or disapproval

Euthanasia Literally meaning a good death, it refers to the practice of hastening someone's death perhaps in order to spare them further suffering

Existentialism A philosophical movement that stresses the uniqueness of each human individual by arguing that existence comes before essence

Extramarital sex Sex outside of marriage, where at least one party is married to someone else; also known as adultery

Globalisation The integration of economies, industries, markets, cultures and policymaking around the world

Hedonistic The idea that pleasure is the true good that should be pursued

Hypothetical imperative A command that is followed to achieve a desired result

Id The instinctive impulses that seek satisfaction in pleasure

Intuitionism The belief that moral values can be defined in terms of some natural property of the world

Legalism Relying too heavily on laws or rules

Maxim The rule that we are following when we perform an action

Naturalism The belief that moral values can be defined in terms of some natural property of the world

Naturalistic fallacy The mistake of defining moral terms with reference to non-moral or natural terms

Non-cognitive The belief that moral statements are not subject to truth or falsity

Non-voluntary euthanasia When a person's life is ended without their consent but with the consent of someone representing their interests, e.g. in PVS cases

Passive euthanasia A treatment is withheld and this indirectly causes the death of the individual

Premarital sex Sex before marriage

Quality of life A largely secular idea that human life has to possess certain attributes in order to have value

Relativism The idea that what is right or wrong is not fixed but is dependent on situation or culture

Rule utilitarianism The idea that we should always follow the rule that generally leads to the greatest balance of good over evil

Sanctity of life A religious concept that human life is made in God's image and is therefore sacred in value

Subjective The idea in ethics that right and wrong depend on the point of view of the individual rather than being decided externally

Superego The internalised ideals from parents and society that tries to make the ego behave morally

Synderesis The inner principle directing a person towards good and away from evil

Teleological The idea that goodness is determined by the outcome of an action

Telos Greek word meaning the purpose or end (as in aim) of something

Utility principle The idea that we should do whatever is useful in terms of increasing overall good and decreasing evil

Voluntary euthanasia When a person's life is ended at their request or with their consent

Whistleblowing When an employee discloses unethical or illegal business practices to the employer or the public

Quiz answers

1 Natural law

1 Aristotle
2 Purpose
3 Reproduce; preserve innocent life; education; live in an ordered society; worship God
4 The Bible
5 Lack of knowledge – they pursue apparent goods
6 Double effect
7 Yes – you only preserve innocent life. Enemy combatants in a just war don't count
8 Eternal law
9 They reject the idea that people have *telos*/purpose
10 To save a woman's life – it is a double effect case

2 Situation ethics

1 *Eros, phileo, storge, agape*
2 Love God with all your heart, soul, mind and strength, and love your neighbour as yourself
3 *Agape*, legalism, antinomianism
4 Pragmatism
5 Pragmatism, positivism, relativism, personalism
6 He says that love is justice distributed
7 It is not – we love our neighbour whether we like them or not
8 He does not see this as a problem. He accepts the point
9 Teleological
10 It is arguably very selective in its interpretation of the words of Jesus

3 Kantian ethics

1 *Summum bonum*. He believes it is necessary as the highest good would require that virtue (good acts) should lead to happiness
2 Categorical imperative
3 Absolutism, deontological
4 Universal law, persons as ends, kingdom of ends
5 Kingdom of ends
6 A rule or principle that we are acting upon
7 Duty
8 A universal law
9 Keeping promises, not committing suicide, not neglecting one's talents, helping others in need
10 Treat people as ends

4 Utilitarianism

1 Hedonic calculus
2 It bases its decisions on the outcome
3 Act utilitarianism
4 Usefulness
5 J.S. Mill
6 Bentham's
7 A weak rule utilitarian may allow a rule to be broken in exceptional circumstances
8 Utilitarians do not consider moral agency – what it is to be the person making such a decision
9 Pleasure and pain
10 The idea that the greatest good lies in satisfying the preferences and interests of as many people as possible

5 Euthanasia

1 Good death
2 Passive euthanasia
3 Peter Singer
4 It prevents doctors from doing something that causes harm to a patient
5 Giving food and water is ordinary. An expensive wonder drug or machine might be extraordinary
6 Joseph Fletcher
7 The concern, if some forms of euthanasia are allowed, that certain worse forms of killing will eventually result
8 Natural law
9 That life is God-given and that it should not be taken by human beings
10 Persistent vegetative state

6 Business ethics

1 Corporate social responsibility
2 Businesses cannot have ethical responsibilities; only individuals can have responsibilities

3 They would probably support whistleblowing (truth-telling and doing the right thing regardless of consequences)

4 They would make a case-by-case decision about whether good was likely to result

5 Consumerism

6 Many people have been lifted out of poverty

7 Kantian ethics

8 Utilitarians may see that there are long-term benefits in behaving ethically as reputations can be lost in minutes

9 Weakness, utilitarian

10 Weakness, Kantian

7 Meta-ethical theories

1 Emotivism

2 Naturalism and intuitionism

3 The idea that something being natural means that it must be good

4 G.E. Moore

5 Naturalism

6 Verification principle

7 Nihilism

8 Normative ethics

9 Emotivism

10 Intuitionism

8 Conscience

1 Synderesis

2 Superego

3 Vincible ignorance is an error for which we are responsible; invincible ignorance is an error where we are not responsible

4 Newman

5 Humanistic

6 A boy's sexual attraction to his mother and resentment of his father

7 Aquinas

8 There is no way that it can be shown to be false

9 Conscientia

10 Dawkins

9 Sexual ethics

1 Non-harm principle

2 Reproduction

3 Pleasure

4 Kant

5 Bring new life (generative) and bring a couple together (uniting)

6 Nothing!

7 Do not commit adultery – a command against extramarital sex

8 Permissible in a loving relationship

9 Bentham and Mill

10 2014

Index